C'NELIA

C'NELIA

CORNELIA WALLACE

A. J. HOLMAN COMPANY

Division of J. B. Lippincott Company
Philadelphia & New York

Lines on page 143 from "I'm an Old Cowhand" quoted by permission. Words and music by Johnny Mercer, copyright 1936 by
Leo Feist, Inc. Copyright renewed 1964. All rights controlled by
the Mercer Music Co.

Photograph on page 33 by Dr. Frederick Stires, Time-Life Picture
Agency, © Time Inc.

Photograph on page 215, bottom, by Sargent

Photograph on page 233, bottom, by Charles Moore

U.S. Library of Congress Cataloging in Publication Data

Wallace, Cornelia, birth date
    C'nelia.

    1. Wallace, Cornelia, birth date 2. Wallace, George
Corley, birth date I. Title.
F330.W28   976.1'06'0924 [B]   75–35835
ISBN–0–87981–047–5

To my mother,
who by her example
taught me the meaning of love

List of Illustrations

I will walk for you if you have no legs.
I will reach for you if you have no arms.
I will speak for you if you are mute.
I will interpret the sounds of the Earth for you if you
are deaf.
I will move your fingers over the shapes of the world if
you are blind.

All these things I will do for you if you ask me to.
But if you should ask me for sympathy, I would give
you none,
For in obliging your wish
I would surely rob you of the spirit to meet the chal-
lenges of life.

C.W.

PART I

Chapter 1

MAY 15, 1972: To say that it began like any Monday morning at the Mansion would not be true. To say that it began like most Mondays since entering the presidential primaries would not quite get it, either.

George was unusually irritable, agitated and fidgety. Everyone who can remember would testify to that fact. But if his edginess was a premonition of the events that would transpire that day, even he could not focus his unsettled feelings into a mental message that could be interpreted as a warning not to make that fateful trip to Maryland.

Several times George had voiced an objection to campaigning at all that Monday. Maryland and Michigan voters would go to the polls on Tuesday, and George doubted that one more day of campaigning would change the outcome of the primary elections in either state. Every politician knows that if you haven't done it by the day before the voters pull the levers, it's too late. The only advantage of last-minute campaigning is the newspaper and television coverage that might leave your name "lingering on the back roads ever gentle on the memory" of the voters' minds for the next twenty-four hours until they are in the polling booths. Then the familiar name triggers the brain's computer and automatically the voter marks his X in the proper column.

There were two nonpsychic, legitimate sources for George's aggravation that day, both female, both Aquarian. One was his second-oldest pretty blond daughter, Peggy Sue; and the other was his second and only living brunette wife, Cornelia.

Peggy Sue had leveled some harsh and unkind words at her father over breakfast. It had happened many times before and amounted to nothing, except that it left both parent and child quite frustrated. Their repeated attempts at communication failed to register a contact. Whenever their dangling wires struck together, the sparks would fly. (I had struck a few of the same wires with George myself.) But theirs was a communication gap filled with love. It never presented itself as a serious threat to their relationship. Therefore, I was not overly concerned about the dissension and considered it a healthy outlet for pent-up emotions. After all, Peggy Sue was finishing her senior year at college, living at home and commuting a hundred miles a day for the privilege. It was obvious that her father enjoyed that arrangement, and I was delighted to have the pleasure of her company. We were not anxious to lose her to marriage or to the world.

The second thorn from the family rosebush stuck George when he came upstairs from breakfast and found "wifey dear" under the hair dryer in the bedroom—with time of departure less than an hour away. I flipped the dryer hood back just in time to catch the full sting and emphasis of the words he hurled at me. "You're going to make me late! If you're not ready, I am going to leave without you."

"I'll be ready by the time you are," I said. George was not yet wearing a hearing aid, so I had learned to pitch and project my voice in such a way that my words never fell on deaf ears. So shrill was my voice I was certain I could not only vibrate his inner ear fluid but, if I chose, could rattle every bone in his body. Doubtless I would have contributed to his deafness had his hearing condition not been caused by a hopeless, predetermined, deteriorative nerve damage.

By the time George reached the bathroom, put a good lather on his morning beard and hit a few strokes with the razor (I don't know why with all that anger he didn't cut his face to ribbons—probably because it was his face), the intercom buzzed. I picked up the phone.

"Mrs. Wallace, Billy Joe Camp is on line twenty-six for the Governor," said the trooper calling from the gate.

"Okay."

I punched line 26. "Billy Joe? Just a minute. The Governor's in the bathroom—I'll have to get him."

"Mrs. Wallace, I need to talk to you, too. The Bonnie Angelo Show in Washington, D.C., called. They'd like to interview you today at two o'clock. You're flying into Washington, so you'd have to go straight to the studio to make it in time. The Governor would have to go on to Wheaton, Maryland. I know you don't like to split up, but you'd have to if you want to do the show."

"Billy Joe, you are the best press secretary the Governor could have and I do hate to interfere with your job, but I've already turned it down."

"Bonnie's a real nice person and her show has a large audience. I think it might help a lot if you'd do it."

"I'd like to oblige you, Billy Joe, but I don't see how I can work it into the schedule. You'd better talk to George. George —George—GEORGE!"

George came shuffling out of the bathroom, still wearing his robe and slippers, with a snarl and traces of lather on his face. I had more respect and better sense than to get too close to an irate Golden Gloves champion even if he is my husband. Clutching my housecoat in one hand and with my other arm fully extended, I handed George the phone.

"Yeah, Billy Joe."

"Governor, you've had several requests for interviews. Some of the reporters want to know if you'll hold a press conference today between your rallies. You don't want to do any of these, do you?"

"No, I don't think that's necessary, do you?"

"No, sir, I don't. All the polls show you way ahead. I don't think you want to hold a press conference and run the risk of an unpleasant interview. There's always a chance of a derogatory headline, and you don't want that on the last day of the campaign."

"No, let's not do that. Is that all?"

"I just want to be sure you have the schedule right on the Wheaton and Laurel rallies."

"I don't know why y'all scheduled those two stops for me today. I've a good mind to cancel."

"I don't think you need to do these two rallies, either, but since they're already set up, I think it would look bad if you canceled out at the last minute."

"I guess you're right, Billy Joe."

"Uh, Governor, I need to speak to Mrs. Wallace again."

"She's not even dressed yet, but here." George shoved the phone back to me.

"Billy Joe," I said, "I don't think I can do the Bonnie Angelo Show—"

Before I could finish the sentence George had commandeered the telephone. "Billy Joe, you just forget about Cornelia doing that show. She's not even going with me today!"

In all the months we had been married, George had never dictated to me, let alone refused to allow me to do anything. I was stunned, but not speechless. "If you think you're going to leave me behind on the last day of the campaign, you've got another thought coming!" I announced.

"Well, you'll see," he said. "I'm not going to wait on you, and if you're not ready, I'm leaving without you!"

I knew he would. The punch in those last words convinced me that his were not idle threats. Until then, I had made every trip with him except for three times when I was forced to stay home: once because of illness, and twice because of personal matters pertaining to the children. My track record was too good to be spoiled this late in the game. I could feel that old Folsom pride swelling up inside me, and I was determined that I would not be left behind on the last day of campaigning. Although breakfast is my favorite meal I had already skipped it. I normally have the "plow-hand's special" every morning—eggs, bacon, grits and butter, hot biscuits and jelly, juice, coffee with lots of cream and sugar, and cereal or grapefruit. That morning I had opted for a clean head of hair instead. Now getting dressed would take precedence over the hairdo.

George and I raced one another to the bathroom. Thanks to Gordon and Alice Persons, our predecessors in the Governor's Mansion, every bathroom in the house had a large tub and a separate, oversized ceramic-tile shower. The Personses were the first official family to occupy the Mansion after my uncle,

Governor James Folsom, purchased it for the state in 1950, and their major contribution was to renovate the antiquated kitchen and bathrooms.

Every morning George and I enjoyed the intimacy of sharing the bath. The luxury of that privacy, a simple joy which most married couples take for granted, was a rare treat for us. The running water provided a backdrop that muffled our exchange of words. Although we traveled together constantly, conversation between us during those trips had practically become a lost art. By land, by air, by sea, there were always at least two security guards present, and while they were loyal, devoted and very close-mouthed, their presence inhibited our discussions of family, friends, enemies or anything else of a personal nature. Having security agents aboard private aircraft never made much sense to me. How could two mortals protect a man from thunderstorms, mechanical failure or pilot error? Airmen choose God for a copilot; I preferred God for a security guard.

Conversation in the family dining room was subject to continuous interruption by members of the staff serving the table. And with four and sometimes five of our six children at home, the bedroom door had long ago become much too thin. My need for privacy was paramount, and although privacy wasn't nonexistent, it was far from abundant. Hence, for me, the bathroom had become a most coveted place. After that Monday, I would be denied even that simple pleasure.

I was dressed and in high gear, racing against the clock. I could make it, I was sure. George was dressed and had gone downstairs to my office to return some telephone calls. Joanne Walker, my personal secretary and lifelong friend, offered to place the calls for him but George insisted on doing it himself. However, when he attempted to dial the first few digits of the number, he was so nervous he knocked the telephone off the desk and into the trash basket. Joanne calmly replaced the phone on the desk as she tried to hide her troubled feeling over George's unusual shaky demeanor. It was fortunate for me that one of the calls pertained to important state business because it allowed me enough time to put some finishing touches on my makeup. Curls were bouncing at random about my head, but

The Alabama Governor's Mansion—bought by my Uncle Jimmy.

Santa and Mrs. Claus
at a P.O.W.-M.I.A.
children's party.

there was no time for teasing. Hairstyling was one talent I had never acquired and did not care to learn.

Not perfectly coiffed, but presentable, I was ready to go. I arrived downstairs just as George was finishing his last call. "I'm ready," I said.

"Let's go."

Joanne managed to smile through her foreboding, "Y'all have a safe trip."

We slipped through the kitchen, out the back door and into the car. Hazel Cain, our cateress, and all the household help were standing in the driveway seeing us off and waving good-bye as they did on each departure.

"Y'all hurry home, Mrs. Wallace. . . . Good luck, Governor."

Not a word passed between us all the way to the airport. The plane, its fuel tanks topped, had been pulled out of the hangar and was waiting for us right where it always was. The pilots were not. Strange, indeed! This had never happened to us before and has never happened to us since. Was this perhaps another subtle indication that we should not make the trip? While we waited in the car, the security men checked out the whereabouts of our missing pilots.

Customarily, the pilots arrive at the airport an hour before each departure to check the weather, check the aircraft and file the required flight plan. The pilots were not at the airport and had not been there at all that morning. The security men made a few phone calls and found the pilots at their motel room—asleep. The Wheaton and Laurel rallies were not reflected on the original campaign schedule as they had been added only the week before—so late that no one had remembered to inform the pilots.

The security men made their report: "Governor, it will be at least another hour before we can depart. Would you like to return to the Mansion? You'd probably be more comfortable there."

"No, boys, thank you. We'll just wait here."

George was not perturbed. A tolerance for other people's mistakes was one of his strong suits. He didn't blame anyone for the delay. He didn't even ask who was responsible for distributing the schedule. He sat silently in his corner, drawing short puffs from his cigar.

I felt slightly triumphant. What with all the fuss George had made over the fact that I was the villainess who was going to make him late, I couldn't resist the opportunity to interject my special brand of humor. "Darling," I said, "I'm so sorry I made you late."

George didn't appreciate my humor and didn't respond. He waited in silence except for an occasional mumbling to himself under his breath.

"I believe I won't go," he said at one point. "I can't go to Michigan and Maryland, too, and one day of stops in Maryland won't make that much difference. If I haven't already won those two primaries, it's too late. I just believe I won't go."

The pilots finally arrived, sputtering their apologies and looking as though they had just wiped the sleep from their eyes. I hoped they had guzzled enough coffee to be fully alert because flying the Jet Commander we used required expert skill and quick reflexes. It was no job for sleepwalkers.

In a few minutes we were ready to leave. As I walked toward the plane, one of the Secret Service agents shook his head in amazement. "Mrs. Wallace, I don't know another man in Governor Wallace's position who would have tolerated this inconvenience without losing his temper."

"Yes, he's pretty special," I said. "He doesn't like to hurt anyone's feelings."

The flight was uneventful. We deplaned at Washington National Airport because it was closest to our destination. The drive to Maryland was pleasant. The traffic was light and the countryside was fresh and green. George was meditating but he did not share his thoughts with me. He was taking short, exaggerated puffs from his cigar almost as if deliberately trying to create a cloud of smoke big enough to hide him and his thoughts from the world. His eyes had a deep, faraway look and I decided not to intrude upon his silence. I glanced over at him several times, hoping for a look that would tell me that he harbored no resentment over our morning squabble. He didn't disappoint me. Sensing my need for a reassuring sign, he looked at me, winked, reached over and squeezed my hand. I smiled and relaxed. It was a tender moment.

Great dreams make great men.

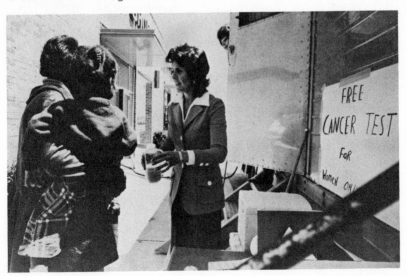

Pushing my pet project.

Chapter 2

WHEATON SHOPPING CENTER was in full view. Despite the fact that the candidate was an hour late, the crowd had not dissipated. Billy Grammer must have played "I've Gotta Travel On" several times with gusto, but thank goodness the people out front didn't heed the lyrics. Naturally I assumed that the people who had waited so long fervently liked my husband. My assumption was far from accurate, as this turned out to be one of the most hostile groups we had ever encountered.

As we drove closer, I noticed that the flatbed trailer truck which we would use as a platform had taken on a new look. Unlike the plain trailer with the simple red and white bunting we had used before at another Maryland shopping center, this one had a high back and wall-like structures running along either side. In many respects, however, the basics of campaigning had not changed much in all my years of political life, which numbered close to thirty at that point. Flatbed trailers are standard props for outdoor rallies. They are movable, hold a lot of weight, seat up to fifty or sixty dignitaries and can usually be borrowed from a local supporter. The back end of the trailer is supported by two double sets of tires, the front by two tubular steel legs with small round steel balls at the base. When the trailer is connected to the cab of a truck, the steel wheels are elevated so that the trailer can be moved. When serving as a platform, wooden blocks are stacked under the steel legs for leveling. Once I was on a flatbed trailer with sixty dignitaries on a hot summer day when the asphalt melted, causing the blocks to turn. The trailer slid off with a sudden loud jolt, but fortunately the platform didn't tilt enough to spill any of its political load. That was literally politics "hot and heavy."

Because of the lateness of our arrival, George got out of the car quickly. I stepped to his rhythm, as I was usually presented first. A phlebitis condition which I had developed made it impossible for me to sit with my knees bent for any length of time, so early in the campaign we had initiated the practice of introducing the First Lady before the Governor. If George had to introduce me after he got into his speech, it broke his timing. Besides, after he appeared on stage, everything else was anticlimactic.

Before I reached the platform, George Mangum, our master of ceremonies, caught up with me and said, "Mrs. Wallace, if you don't mind, we'd prefer you didn't go out on the stage this time. That's a pretty rough crowd."

"Mind?" I said. "Not at all. Thanks for the favor. With this head of hair, the last thing I want is to be seen."

Extra security men formed a line on either side of George, shielding him until he was behind the bulletproof podium. Then they stood around the platform, facing the crowd. Without our knowledge Billy Joe Camp had already taken the precaution of removing the four-inch box George usually stood on. None of his body was exposed except his head, the most vital part of a man. Why had no one ever thought of bulletproof glass for the top part of that podium?

Objects came flying through the air, all in George's direction. The two security men closest to him were doing an excellent job of intercepting the barrage of articles that were hurled at him because none hit the intended target. Eggs and tomatoes usually were the favorites of these frustrated discus throwers who failed to qualify for the Olympics, but on this day I deduced that most of what was being thrown was wadded-up balls of paper. Later I learned that I deduce about as well as I balance a checkbook. Actually, the white balls were bars of soap embedded with nails, sharp ends protruding. I thought stoning had gone out of style shortly after Christ. Evidently with certain groups it's still stylish—only it's called

Winning the 1972 Florida primary was the sweetest victory.

When campaigning, two hands are better than one.

"soaping." The scene reminded me of the time when George was hit over the head in 1968 with a sign that read, "God Is Love."

George cut his speech short. We had almost two hours before the next rally, so we drove on to our holding rooms at the Howard Johnson Motel in Laurel. I immediately inquired about getting my hair combed. The telephone operator at the motel was kind enough to check some nearby shops only to find most of them were closed on Mondays. She found one open: the Montgomery Ward beauty salon near the Laurel Shopping Center.

"This is the Howard Johnson Motel in Laurel, Maryland," the operator said. "Mrs. George Wallace is a guest here. Could you work her in for a comb-out? No, she doesn't need a shampoo and set, just a comb-out."

The hairdresser, Ed Pelky, thought she was joking. "The Mrs. George Wallace from Alabama?" he asked.

"Yes. Can you take her at two o'clock? She needs to be at a rally at three P.M. at the Laurel Shopping Center."

"Sure, we can take her. Hey, and while you're at it, how about sending Pat Nixon, too?"

At 1:30 P.M. we went down the hall to a room where the motel manager had asked our whole entourage to be his guests at a midday banquet. He served all of George's favorite dishes and before George's plate he had placed the familiar bottle of ketchup and a full glass of milk. The manager had gone to a lot of trouble to make us feel at home, which we appreciated very much.

The banquet was an unusually generous gesture on the part of our host since our group was so large. Our party included my husband and me, Billy Joe Camp, two Alabama security men, two Maryland state troopers and twenty Secret Service agents. Many of the agents had requested George's detail because some of them had traveled with him in 1968 and admired him very much. One of them said, "It's impossible to work for the man and not love him." The feeling was mutual and for George it extended to all personnel of law enforcement. He knew that any one of them would lay down his life for him. Later that night I would think about George and the men who shared that meal with him, and it would remain forever fixed in my memory as a symbolic last supper.

My beauty-parlor appointment was drawing near. I excused myself, assured my husband that I would return in time to accompany him to the rally, gave him a big kiss on the cheek and departed. A trooper with the Maryland State Police volunteered to drive me to Montgomery Ward's since no one in our party was familiar with the area. It took longer to get there than I had anticipated, which meant I would probably be late for the Laurel rally. So what if I was? The biggest rally was scheduled for Annapolis at 8 P.M., and if I missed the Laurel rally altogether at least I would look good that night.

Ed Pelky, the hairdresser, decided the set I had given myself that morning was not good enough to hold a tease, so he elected to use the hot rollers. Waiting for the rollers to heat would take even longer and I was sure I would not make the rally, but the result was worth the wait because my hair looked terrific. I doubt that Ed could have done any better even if he had known that a week later that hairdo would appear on the cover of *Life* magazine.

The trooper had waited patiently. "I've got five minutes to get to that rally. Can we hurry?" I said.

"Yes, ma'am!" Feeling obliged to deliver me safely into the hands of my protectors, the trooper headed toward the Howard Johnson Motel. It was exactly 3 P.M.

"Let's go straight to the shopping center," I suggested. "I'm sure they've already left the motel."

"They may be waiting for you," the trooper said. "I think we should check the motel to be sure."

"I'm certain they won't wait for me. George would never be late for a rally."

"Well, we're almost there, so let's just go by and make sure."

The motorcade was gone. The trooper parked the patrol car and went inside. He was back in two seconds flat. "They're all gone. I thought surely they would have waited for you."

"Well, you see," I explained, "I'm not the one who has to make the speech. And I'm sure they aren't worried about me. They know they left me in good hands."

26

When we reached the Laurel Shopping Center, George was fifteen minutes into his speech. The platform had the same plywood back its counterpart in Wheaton had sported earlier in the day but had no side walls. It had been positioned in front of the bank building in the middle of the parking lot. The trooper parked the car alongside the Secret Service motorcade. I waited in the car for a moment, surveying the crowd and trying to decide how I could slip behind the platform without distracting the audience with my belated arrival. The motorcade and backdrop provided sufficient screening for me to pass through the crowd without causing any commotion. When I reached the back of the platform our sound engineer, Derryl Gordon, greeted me in a loud voice.

"Hey, Mrs. Wallace. Where've you been?"

"Getting my hair combed," I whispered, hoping he'd take the hint. Although his workers were not aware of it, George became very annoyed if members of the road crew laughed or talked loudly while his speech was in progress. Since he spoke extemporaneously, any disruption could cause him to lose his train of thought. The only hint he ever gave that anyone had fallen into his disfavor was an occasional aside, "I didn't see any of you clapping," which I knew really meant, Why weren't you all paying attention to me? I guess George forgot that all of us had heard that speech more than a hundred times. No one meant to be disrespectful, but occasionally the idle chitchat we engaged in got out of hand.

In spite of our human failings, none of us ever really tired of hearing that speech, and most of us prided ourselves that any one of us could probably give it if the occasion ever demanded. Whenever George added a new line to his remarks, we all told him whether we did or didn't like it, even though he never solicited our critique. If he struck a responsive chord with the crowd, that told him all he needed to know. He was a master of his trade.

As I peered from behind the backdrop, I could see lines of policemen in every direction. They were members of the Prince George's County Police, Prince George's County Sheriff's Department, Laurel Police Department and Maryland State Police. The plainclothes officers mingled with the crowd. It was the largest number of law-enforcement officers used to ensure my husband's safety since the beginning of the 1972 campaign.

After the Wheaton hostilities, I'm sure they thought they would be needed, but it appeared that they wouldn't see any action this afternoon. Laurel, Maryland, had turned out the warmest, friendliest crowd I had ever seen. No demonstrators were visible. The sun was shining and the brightness of the day added to the warm atmosphere generated by the local people. I was basking in the sun and feeling good because this rally was such a contrast to the earlier one.

As I listened to George's words over the loudspeaker system, I noticed that his usually powerful voice was becoming scratchy. It was getting weaker so rapidly that I was sure he wouldn't be able to talk at all in a few minutes. Mere water wouldn't revive his strained vocal cords. What to do? I remembered that one of my grandmother's home remedies for a hoarse throat was a spoonful of honey. Over the tops of the cars I could see a grocery store. I turned to Ed Wesson, a member of our road crew, who stood beside me. "Quick, Ed, run over there and buy me a jar of honey as fast as you can."

"Honey? What for?" Ed asked.

"For the Governor's throat. Hurry, hurry!"

Each word was getting drier and thinner. Ed was back so fast he could have run into himself coming and going. Derryl Gordon handed me a Styrofoam cup. I tore off the top of the container, filled the bottom of the cup with honey and gave it to Ed. "Here, take this to the Governor and tell him to drink it."

George had stopped talking and had stepped away from the microphone. Ed walked on stage and handed George the cup. "What is that?" he said.

"Honey," Ed explained. "Your wife said to drink it."

George resumed his speech with all of his full volume and resonance. The power of his voice was augmented as quickly as it had diminished. He had not, however, partaken of the honey.

I had two hands full of sticky fingers. Maybe the bank had a bathroom. The doors were locked, but I rapped on the glass until someone let me in, and after I explained my dilemma, a lady in a blue dress led me to a lavatory.

"I wanted to meet your husband," she said, "but I had to work."

"I'm sure he'll shake hands today. If you will come to the door when he stops speaking, I'll come over and get you so you can meet him."

I went back and waited for George to finish his speech. He concluded shortly and descended a set of steps in the middle of the platform. Two women from the Laurel campaign headquarters stopped him on the steps and kissed him on each cheek. Agent Michael Wiles and I walked toward him, both of us trying to anticipate his next move. Would he or would he not shake hands?

George turned to his right and started toward the cars. Agent Wiles was halfway to the motorcade when George stopped. He had changed his mind. He peeled off the coat to his suit, folded it once and hung it over the arm of one of the three agents flanking him. He went directly to the crowd on his far left, even though a politician shaking hands usually works a crowd from right to left because it is more natural since Americans always shake with their right hand. The people were so excited over the prospect of touching him that they held their hands high in the air.

George was wearing a light-blue short-sleeved shirt. He raised his bare arms and with both his hands open clasped the eager voters, two hands at a time. It was a habit of mine to shake hands directly in front of or behind him, so I moved closer to take my place at his side. By this time George was completely obscured from my view by Agent Jimmy Taylor on his right, Agent Nick Zarvos at his back, and Captain E. C. Dothard, Alabama state trooper and head of the Governor's personal security detail, on his left. Laurens Pierce and his CBS television crew were between Taylor and Zarvos. I had never had any trouble finding a small opening to squeeze through, but Laurens Pierce, with his shoulder camera and his sound man, made it impossible for me to follow my usual routine.

I was standing four feet directly behind George and the circle of men that surrounded him. Realizing I couldn't get closer, I stood contemplating how I could be more effective in helping him campaign. Someone took my hand and said, "Hi, I'm Dora Thompson." It was one of the women who had kissed George on the steps. While she was talking to me, my mind flashed to the lady in the blue dress at the bank. I must keep my promise. By the time I could fetch her, George would be finished with the line of people and would probably be near the bank. I could join him then. I saw the lady in the blue dress waiting on the steps. I took four steps. . . .

Bang-bang-bang, bang-bang!

It was 3:58 P.M.

It would be as impossible to recapture that moment on paper as it would be to suspend time, but it seemed that day as if time did stop. For one minute after the shots were fired everything was like exaggerated slow motion. And yet, all my mental and physical reactions actually took place in a split second. All my senses sharpened. My naturally quick reflexes seemed supernatural.

Firecrackers, I thought. But no one would dare shoot firecrackers! I wheeled to my left. George was lying on the ground flat on his back, a large red bloodstain on his right side above the waist. My first impression was: No fatal wound. The next thought that flashed in my mind was: They'll finish him off while he's lying on the ground!

There was no one near George so I rushed to him and fell over him, trying to cover his head and his heart with my body.

Chapter 3

THE WOUNDED BODY of George Wallace lay on the black asphalt parking lot of the Laurel, Maryland, shopping center. Only the crimson stain on his right side gave any indication that his motionless form might hold any traces of life. The casual observer surely would have placed odds against his survival.

The air was humid and oppressive. The sun blazed down as if out of its warmth it could supply life-giving energy to my husband's body. I pressed my cheek hard against George's face. There were no more shots. Feeling confident that he was sufficiently protected, I lifted my head to speak to him. His eyes held a fixed stare of shock and disbelief.

"George, George! Are you all right?" I cried.

His eyes began to focus. He looked as if he were afraid to move. I began to cry with shaking sobs. George did not speak. I pressed my lips to his mouth as if to kiss the life back into his body.

His voice was expressionless as he answered, "I'm shot. I've been shot."

The sound of his first words hushed my sobs and stopped my tears. I slipped my arm under his head in an effort to cushion him from the gravel-studded ground.

"It's over! I'm taking you home!" I told him. I meant, We're through with politics. We're going home to be with our children as a family, once and for all.

I was constantly faced with the choice of staying home and

being with my children or traveling and being with my husband. There was little opportunity for all of us to be together. I had tried staying home, then tried going on the road. Either way I was miserable. Something was always missing. Even I did not realize how important this longing for my misplaced home life was to me or how repressed were my inner conflicts until I blurted out those words: "It's over. I'm taking you home!"

Suddenly, in the midst of this disaster, I visualized an end to my personal frustration. At last I would have my husband and my children at home together. What those words told me about myself! I had caught a fleeting glimpse before, but had pushed it deep down again because there had seemed no possible solution without interfering with my husband's career. Rather than bear the guilt of holding him back from his lifelong goals and ambitions, I had chosen to sacrifice my own dreams. But now my husband's dream was dashed to the ground and, ironically, out of his tragedy it seemed my emotional needs might be met at last.

Such a silly, romantic notion some women entertain: a white frame house, a picket fence and the fragrance of honeysuckle floating in every window! I suppose it's a common malady among young girls who reached their impressionable teens in the 1950s as I did. Most of us spent every Sunday afternoon at the local picture show watching B musicals and having refrains of "My Blue Heaven" and "Singin' in the Rain" etched on our memories until, putting them together, we formed an unrealistic picture of what our life should be whenever we got old enough to enjoy it.

But this was no time for indulging in daydreams and fantasies. The images lingered for a moment, then faded as I thanked the Lord that my husband was still alive. My mind was set on getting George well, taking him home and getting him out of politics.

"Darling, are you all right?" I asked again.

"I can't move my legs," he said. If my ears heard those words my mind rejected them. Of course he can't move his legs, I rationalized. Anyone who was shot like this couldn't possibly move.

All around I saw trousered legs closing in on us. Now some of them were kneeling. A few of the faces took shape. I recog-

Greater love hath no man than this . . . *(John 15:13)*

nized Jimmy Taylor on the other side of George, appraising the only apparent wound. Shouts began to go up from all around. "Somebody get a doctor!"

"Somebody call an ambulance."

As bewildered people crowded around George, Billy Grammer and George Mangum used the public-address system to try to restore order. "Move back, people, please—if you love the Governor, move back and give him some air!"

"Let me through, I'm a doctor." As a disheveled elderly gentleman broke through the barrier of people, Jimmy Taylor's eyes darted from me to the man, then back to me. I knew Jimmy had doubts of his own or he wouldn't have looked at me for approval. I answered his mute question with my eyes. No, I was not sure the man was a doctor. Every stranger had become a potential assassin. Jimmy demanded identification and proof that the man was a physician. His credentials seemed in order.

I studied the doctor's movements as if I were a veteran O.R. supervisor and he a junior intern. He unfolded a white handkerchief and placed it over George's open wound. It didn't look like much for a bandage. (Later I was told it was a method of detecting a suction motion that would have indicated a punctured lung.)

The doctor was soon spared my critical eyes as I was abruptly lifted to my feet by two strong, firm hands. Someone was pulling me away from George's body. What in the world? I struggled unsuccessfully to free the hold as tears began streaming down my face. "What are you doing? Let me go! Don't, please! Let me go!"

It was Agent Bill Breen pulling me to my feet. "Mrs. Wallace, please, I'm supposed to take care of you," he said.

"Please, don't keep me away from my husband. Please let me stay with him."

Agent Breen surrendered to my pleading and released me. I quickly resumed my position near George's head. Agent Breen joined me, knelt down and felt George's pulse.

"Who are you?" George asked him.

"I'm a Secret Service agent, Governor."

"Well, you can put your gun up. I've been shot enough for one day."

34

"Oh, my goodness!" Agent Breen gasped. He had drawn his gun instinctively when the first shots were fired and had never returned it to his holster.

"George, are you all right?" I asked him.

"I'm all right. Go see about Dothard."

I hadn't noticed that Captain Dothard lay a few feet from George. Meady Hilyer, Alabama security, was supporting his head. His face was red and his breathing was tight and forced. He had a wound across his stomach, but I couldn't estimate the damage. At that moment I thought his condition was much more critical than George's.

"Dothard, how are you?" I asked.

"I'm all right," he said. "Don't worry about me. Look after the Governor."

It seemed like an eternity since I had rushed to George when I first saw him on the ground. Why hadn't the ambulance arrived? Had anybody called one? A frightening realization came to me: My husband might die here on the ground because we weren't able to get him to a hospital. I began to sob again. "Get an ambulance—somebody please get an ambulance," I screamed. Panic gripped all of us as we simultaneously sensed the urgent need for immediate medical attention.

"Take him on!" the doctor shouted.

Captain Dothard had raised himself up on one elbow and was shouting and waving orders. "Move him! Move him! Get him out of here!"

"Get the station wagon!" shouted Byron Prescott, an Alabama security man. I scrambled along beside George as several men lifted him and carried him toward the wagon.

"Easy! Easy now. Careful." They pulled him gently onto the floor of the station wagon. Before they had loosed their hold, the Laurel, Maryland, Rescue Squad ambulance had arrived. It was exactly 4:05 P.M. The seven minutes since those shots had rung out seemed like forever.

I relinquished my place by George's side so those trained in emergency techniques could have the vantage point. The Rescue Squad worked calmly and quickly. Skillfully they placed George and Dothard on stretchers and started toward the van-type ambulance.

I climbed up into the back of the ambulance as the attendants were loading the stretchers. There was nowhere to sit so I made a place on a narrow black box behind the driver's seat. Billy Joe Camp and campaign aide Emmett Eaton crowded in next to me. David Golden of Alabama security got in front between James Mills, the ambulance driver, and Darryl Duckworth, another attendant. When the stretchers were positioned, Barbara Luber and Jon Fiedler, two members of the Rescue Squad, stationed themselves next to the wounded men and initiated first-aid procedures. Agents James Mitchell, Miller Davis and Jimmy Taylor wedged themselves in between the cots. All told there were thirteen people crammed into the ambulance.

Another member of the Rescue Squad tried to climb into the rear of the ambulance along with the agents, but before he was all the way in, Byron Prescott, not knowing who he was, grabbed him by the seat of the pants and pulled him out.

As soon as the van was loaded, the ambulance lurched forward. The motion of the vehicle caused the doors to fly open, and both stretchers slid toward the opening. All of us in the back grabbed at the cots and stopped them from rolling out as we shouted for the driver to stop. The driver and the attendant in the front got out and went to the back of the van. The doors had come open because our legs had taken up so much room the stretchers had not been placed far enough into the ambulance. The attendants pulled the stretchers out, then shoved them farther back. As George's stretcher jammed against my shinbones with the full force and weight of his body, I winced in pain and bit my lip to keep from crying out. Remembering what Dr. Evan Shute had told me when I saw him in London, Ontario—"Be careful not to injure your legs because a blood clot could be fatal"—I shuddered to think what a blow like that could do to my recurring phlebitis condition. The doors were finally securely locked and the ambulance started again.

The siren started wailing and the ambulance moved slowly through the crowd in the parking lot. Stricken with grief and concern, people crowded around the ambulance, pushing and shoving from every side, as if the ambulance, like some giant sponge, might absorb and carry them along with their hero.

We left the shopping center, and as the driver turned onto a narrow street he carefully increased the speed. There was no residential area and no town—just cars, occasional buildings and streets that seemed to lead nowhere. The only familiar landmark was the nearby shopping center where earlier in the day I had had my hair combed.

The traffic was not heavy, but it was not light either. A few cars pulled over to get out of the way, but we were going around most of them before they could get off the road. I wished for the streets to be deserted. Why should I expect them to be? Why should I expect the traffic to be any different from a normal day in Laurel?

The driver made several turns, then headed down a straight, two-lane paved street, weaving in and out of traffic. The ambulance seemed to lift off two wheels every time it veered around an automobile. Even with so many bodies aboard, the weight didn't seem sufficient to keep it from leaning as it turned and worked its way toward a destination known only to God and the Rescue Squad. I certainly didn't know where we were going or even if we were going in the right direction. First I thought we were going one way, then it seemed we were going another way. I had lost all sense of direction—usually one of my better senses and one that I frequently relied on in unfamiliar environs. Without it I began to feel helpless. My earlier fear that George would die on the ground was now replaced by my fear that he would die in the ambulance before we reached the hospital. Later I learned that the ambulance crew actually had started for Leland Memorial Hospital but had changed their minds in favor of Holy Cross.

One thing for sure, I hated the design of that van. The weight distribution was wrong and the frame was too high off the ground. Oh, for a good, old-fashioned 1950 Cadillac ambulance! I used to wonder why anyone would be so extravagant as to purchase such an expensive ambulance when sick people are too ill to care whether they are carried to the hospital in style. Now I knew why. It was not for appearance's sake but because the body weight of a heavier ambulance kept it from turning over.

The trip seemed longer and longer. There was one thing I knew for certain: the hospital was not just around the corner and a few blocks down the street. Up front David Golden was shouting at the driver, "Can't you drive this thing any faster?

If you can't, I can!" and he rested his hands on the pistol in his holster. He looked as if he would swallow the driver whole, shove him out the door or sit in his lap and squash him flat as he prepared to defend his challenge to take the wheel.

I poked the driver on the shoulder. "Hurry. Please hurry!"

David and I stopped our verbal and physical assaults on the driver but David did not withdraw his threat to take the wheel.

The traffic thinned and we picked up speed. Beyond the left side of the ambulance I could see a four-lane highway. I looked out the front window and saw that the driver was approaching the ingress full speed ahead and siren wide open. This was one driver who didn't want David Golden in his lap and he had no intention of slowing down. Someone had better play lookout. David and I went from tormentors to protectors in one swift second, and it was well that we did. I could see the cab of a high transfer truck. Swiftly the body of the truck filled the view from my window—as we say down South, "He was hauling dirt." The truck driver didn't see us and I knew he couldn't hear us because his diesels were making as much noise as our sirens, if not more. I tried desperately to flag him away as David leaned over our driver, joining my futile efforts to get the truck driver to move over. Our driver's foot never lifted from the accelerator. Neck and neck we went right up the ramp. I held my breath and closed my eyes as we squeezed in front of the truck at the very last second.

One of the volunteer attendants, Barbara Luber, was busy administering first aid to George. She had taken his blood pressure, checked the open wound in his side and bandaged some flesh wounds she found in his right arm. George refused her attempts to get him to breathe oxygen. When she tried to place the mask over his face he moved his head from side to side.

"George, take the oxygen. Take the oxygen," I said.

He took a few whiffs, then shook the mask off. "It's hot in here. Open the window," he said. When no one obeyed him, he reached over, unlatched the window and flipped it outward. He didn't lock it open at the hinges and it flapped in the wind. Barbara Luber repeated her attempts to administer the oxygen and I continued to encourage George to oblige her. She eventually succeeded in giving intermittent doses.

The revolving red light flashed on top of the Rescue Squad

ambulance as it sped rapidly along the Washington, D.C., Beltway, the same highway George and I had traveled only a few hours ago from the airport. I learned later that this same Laurel Rescue Squad had taken first place in the National Rescue Squad Championship.

Radio reports had gone out from the scene of the shooting, broadcasting the news that George Wallace had been shot. None reported his condition because no one knew, and at that moment I did not know either. But my faith was strong. It had always sustained me and I trusted it to sustain me now. In spite of myself, the tears and sobs came again. Would it be too late? "God, please don't let him die," I prayed.

For the first time since the hot lead bullets had pierced his flesh and racked his body, George was beginning to experience pain. "Ooooooo . . . oh . . . ooooooooh, give me something," he moaned. "Can't you give me something?"

"We're almost there, Governor." Barbara Luber tried to comfort him. "Breathe deep."

"I can't stand it! Can't you give me something?"

I turned to the driver. "How much farther is it?"

"Not far. You should be able to see the hospital over there on the right."

"Where?"

"There! The building with the cross in front of it. That's Holy Cross Hospital."

And there it was. George would have his hour of destiny at the foot of the cross, I thought. His life would be in God's hands. The Lord giveth and the Lord taketh away—as he sees fit, when he sees fit. *It is he that hath made us, and not we ourselves; we are his people, and the sheep of his pasture.*

The hospital was across an open field from us; the Silver Spring exit was down the road. Why was it taking so long?

"Knock me out!" George pleaded with us. "Please, knock me out. I don't mind dying, but please don't make me suffer like this!"

We turned off the Beltway and made several more turns. I was beginning to wish we had carried George across the field.

"Governor, we're here," the driver said with obvious joy. He had handled his job well and he knew it. He had had a successful run. All his passengers were alive.

Chapter 4

WE PULLED into the emergency driveway. I could see the doors
of the hospital. I determined then and there that if anyone put
an admission form in front of me, I would shove it down his
throat. I looked frantically for a doctor but didn't see one, although I learned later that a doctor was standing there in shirt-
sleeves and pants, but no white coat. I did see a nurse clutching
a clipboard to her bosom.

The Lord must love her, too, because she kept that clipboard smack against her chest, and if she had any admission
forms, I didn't see them. I think she was there to show us the
way to the emergency room, but the Rescue Squad had
George's stretcher out of the ambulance and inside the building
before she could shift her weight and get her starting foot off
the ground.

I saw a number of men in green scrub suits in the hallway
beside the entrance. When we reached them, some of them
took Dothard in one direction, and the others took George into
a small emergency room. I followed. The room was made even
smaller by doctors, nurses and technicians. There was one spe-
cialist for every part of the body, including a neurosurgeon, a uro-
surgeon and three cardiovascular surgeons. Each one had
passed five reviewing boards to be eligible to serve on the staff
of the hospital. The standards were very high.

One of the surgeons was a patient recuperating from surgery
when the emergency code was sent out over the speaker system
in Holy Cross Hospital. The interpretation of the code was:
"Any and all physicians needed in the emergency room." He

was already wearing a green surgical suit, since he found hospital gowns too high at the neck and too drafty at the bottom, and upon hearing the alert and realizing that a human life might depend on his skill, he pulled the large intravenous needle from his arm, removed his indwelling Foley catheter, got up from his sickbed and reported to the emergency room. His colleagues commended him for so conscientiously adhering to the Hippocratic oath and sent him back to his room immediately.

I stood just inside the door and watched as George was moved from the ambulance stretcher to the examining table under the big light.

"Everybody get out of here," said Dr. Joseph Schanno, the attending physician. "The room's too small and there's not enough air for the patient to breathe."

Some people left. Others—I was one of them—were asked to leave. I stood outside the door and hugged the frame. No one knew who I was—it didn't matter. A green-suited man with large, brown, doleful eyes allowed me to go back into the room. The doctors were having trouble getting George's shirt off. When they tried to tear it, it would not rip. Taking up a pair of scissors, one doctor turned to another and said, "This is an expensive shirt. I'll bet it cost fifteen dollars if it cost a penny."

A portable X-ray unit was ordered. Vital signs were checked and a chest surgeon was listening to George's heartbeat. George was conscious and talking.

Someone finally realized I was the patient's wife and started asking me questions about George's medical history. Was he allergic to any drugs? Yes, one: sulfa. What time did he have his last food? Two o'clock. How much did he eat? Everything on his plate. The doctors looked at each other and shook their heads.

"Is that bad?" I asked.

"Well, let's just put it this way: If you're going to be shot in the stomach, it would be better not to have eaten."

The physical examination continued. "Check his reflexes," one doctor instructed. The doctors moved his legs, flexed his knees and put them down flat. Everyone in the room was busy doing whatever he was trained to do. There was a constant bustle of activity.

"Governor, move your legs," Dr. Schanno said. "Governor, move your legs."

Every green-clad body in the room became as still as the legs on which their eyes focused.

"He can't hear you," I said, looking about the room apologetically. "He has a bad hearing problem." They didn't know how to make him hear, but he would hear me. I gave my voice that special pitch. "George, move your legs."

His legs didn't move. "I can't," George said. "I've been shot in the spine."

His trousers were lowered to the top of his thighs. One of the doctors began a series of skin pricks with a pin, beginning four inches below his waist and moving at two-inch intervals down his thigh. I knew what a neurological exam meant. As the pin pierced his flesh George offered no physical or verbal response. He didn't feel any of it. His legs didn't move. He didn't even flinch. He didn't move his legs because he couldn't. He was paralyzed. I looked into the doctor's eyes. He looked back at me hard and straight, silently confirming the obvious diagnosis. It was a sobering realization.

So much for my dream—George's recovery would not be that simple. It was to be a complicated, drawn-out period of adjustment for both of us, with always the demon of self-pity to battle. The romantic notions of home life and contented bliss would have to go back on the shelf, for I could ill afford the luxury of fulfilling my own selfish wishes. That would put the priorities out of order. I resolved that I would suppress my emotions and I would shed my tears alone, but never in front of George.

The portable X-ray machine was placed into position to X-ray the spine. The pictures were made and returned in a matter of minutes. The film revealed a bullet in the spinal canal at the level of the first lumbar vertebra.

George would need a reason to live. The knowledge of his paralysis, with all its psychological ramifications, would be too much to cope with on top of the terrible fact that someone had tried to kill him and almost succeeded. To lose the use of his legs would make life difficult, but to lose the motivating force in his life—politics—would make life impossible. He had to have that motivating force. To take him home crippled and to take him out of politics—I might as well have left him to die on the ground at that shopping center. There are different ways for a man like George Wallace to die; one is to die physically, and the other is to die politically. I was not sure George could separate the latter from the former.

Governor Marvin Mandel of Maryland had received the news of the attack on George minutes after the incident took place. He immediately boarded a jet helicopter stationed on the grounds of the State Capitol in Annapolis. Shortly after we arrived at Holy Cross Hospital I was informed the Governor was already en route. The doctors were still evaluating George's injuries when a very distressed-looking Governor Mandel came briskly down the corridor. I met him halfway down the hall.

Governor Mandel's was the first familiar face I saw in that Maryland hospital full of strangers. Marvin and Barbara Mandel had struck up a warm relationship with George and me at the various governors' conferences we all had attended. Barbara and I had an instant liking for each other, and I always looked forward to seeing her. Now I was especially grateful to see Governor Mandel. I understood his distress. Since the Kennedy assassinations, public appearances by a President and presidential candidates create a certain amount of apprehension in those who are responsible for their safety. President Nixon's trip to Mobile and Birmingham, Alabama, had caused George much anxiety. More than once he had remarked, "I hope nothing happens to him while he's in my state. Take every precaution to ensure his safety. I'll be so relieved when I know he's out of Alabama safe and unharmed." Texas seemed a little tainted after John Kennedy was shot in Dallas because some people considered the act a reflection of the character of the people who live there, even though Lee Harvey Oswald was not a Texan. I knew Governor Mandel was sincerely concerned about the effect the incident would have on the image of his state. I knew he was also worried about his friend and colleague.

"I left as soon as I heard the news," Governor Mandel said. "This is a terrible thing! How is George?"

"I think he's all right, Governor."

"What can I do for you?"

Holy Cross Hospital was an unfamiliar place to me. At that time I had no way of knowing how competent the medical staff was or how well the hospital was equipped. The injuries were so massive I knew George needed the best doctors. In Alabama I would have known what to do, where to go and who to call. Who in Maryland would know? The Governor of the state, of course, and there he was, standing in front of me, asking, "What can I do for you?"

"Get me the best doctors in your state," I said.

"I'll take care of it," he said as he squeezed my hand.

Reassured and confident, I reentered the small emergency room to find a new atmosphere of urgency.

Dr. Schanno looked over at me. "Mrs. Wallace, your husband's blood pressure has suddenly dropped," he said. "We're going to have to go in right away and take a look. We suspect his liver has been damaged."

I looked at the doctor sternly. "You do whatever is necessary to save his life."

"Let's go," another doctor said. His words had barely reached my ears when George was wheeled swiftly past me. The doctors and nurses made a mass exit and I tried in vain to catch up. Down the corridor the entourage moved. I lost sight of them when they turned right at the emergency entrance where we had first brought George into the hospital. Fearful that I would lose my way, I quickened my pace. They were already at the end of a deserted corridor twice as long as the first one. They pushed through a pair of swinging doors at the far end and into the operating section of the hospital. By the time I reached the area, George had been taken into a large rectangular room across from a nurses' station. The chrome-lighted room was light beige from floor to ceiling. Oxygen tanks were scattered about the room. It was the recovery room, not the operating room. It was being used to prep George. An I.V. was already being administered. Most of the surgeons had gone into another area to scrub.

There was one other patient in the room. A nurse approached me and said, "Mrs. Wallace, would you come and

44

speak to this lady? She was at the shopping center with your husband. She was shot in the leg."

"Oh, no!" I said. "You mean someone else was shot? I didn't know. Of course I'll speak to her. What's her name?"

"Dora Thompson. Mrs. Thompson, this is Mrs. Wallace."

I didn't recognize Dora without her red-white-and-blue costume and Wallace hat. I'm not sure I would have recognized her anyhow because all the time we had been talking at the shopping center I was looking at the people surrounding George and trying to figure out how I could squeeze between them to shake hands alongside him. I had left Dora standing in the same spot where we had been talking. If she had walked off and I had remained, in all probability the bullet that had entered her leg would have hit me.

"Oh, Mrs. Wallace, how is Governor Wallace?" Dora Thompson asked. "I can't believe this happened to him. I was holding your hand, talking to you, right before it happened."

"He's going to be all right, Dora. How are you doing?"

"I'm doing fine. Governor Wallace has got to make it. He's just got to!" Tears filled her eyes.

"He'll be all right. I know he will." I turned away from Dora and back to George. He was prepped and ready for surgery, and no longer conscious of the pain. I was glad. About that time a nurse came in and said, "Mrs. Wallace, the President is calling you."

I hesitated because I didn't want to leave George. He had heard what the nurse had said. "Honey, you'll have to go talk to the President."

I was ushered into a private office. When I picked up the phone the President was on the line.

"I regret this terrible thing that has happened to your husband, but he is a strong man and I know he will come through this."

"Yes, sir," I said, "he's doing fine. He's going into surgery now."

"I've asked my personal physician, Dr. Lukash, to be with you tonight. If you need any assistance let him know. Tell the Governor we'll be keeping a check on him," the President said.

"I'll tell him. Thank you, very much, Mr. President."

When I went back, the nurses were taking George to surgery. I walked beside him as they rolled him past the double doors and out of the recovery room. On the left was the nurses' station, on the right a tiny office with a door and a plate-glass window, and at an angle to the left, behind another set of double doors, was the operating room. I followed George to the last set of double doors.

"You're going to be all right, darling. Everything's going to be fine," I said as he was pushed inside the operating room.

As the doors swung closed, panic gripped me. Separation had been a problem for me ever since my father died. I couldn't bear to be separated from people I loved—especially George at this critical time. I clung to the door frame as I tried to control the emotions that seemed to burst inside me.

One of the doctors stood between me and the door. I turned to him and pleaded, "Please, can I go in?"

"No, Mrs. Wallace, you can't go in there." He was kind and gentle.

"Oh, please, please, let me go in! I'll be all right. I have to know how he is."

"I'm sorry, you can't go in there. We'll keep you informed as the surgery progresses. We'll let you know everything, Mrs. Wallace. As soon as we know we'll send you word."

The doctor then introduced me to a nurse supervisor and told me that she would come out from time to time and report on George's condition. I failed to convince him that I could keep my composure if he allowed me to go in the operating room. He knew what the procedure would be, and now that I know what took place in that room during the surgery, I'm sure I would have fainted had I witnessed it.

I was taken into the tiny office with the plate-glass window opposite the operating room and facing the nurses' station, where there was a small desk and chair. A lady in street clothes offered me her chair, but I couldn't sit down. I paced back and forth, up and down the hall between the tiny office and the operating-room doors. Would I take some food, a Coke, coffee? No, I wasn't hungry, I wasn't thirsty, I wasn't anything. I was just there. I didn't need anything except to know George was all right.

My emotional balance hung on the scales with George's

life—the two of us on one end, fate on the other. If he lived, I would be okay. If he didn't I knew I would fall into a million pieces right there on the hospital floor and someone would have to sweep me up with a broom and a dustpan. I doubted that anyone would ever be able to put all my pieces back together again.

My thoughts were interrupted when Billy Joe Camp informed me that Agent Nick Zarvos had also been injured at the shopping center and had been rushed to another hospital.

A Catholic priest approached me and introduced himself. "I'm Father Fortin. I'm the hospital chaplain."

"Hello, Father. I'm so glad you're here."

"Would you like to go to the chapel and pray?"

"Yes, Father, I'd like that very much."

I followed the priest to a chapel on the main floor of the hospital. Father Fortin went to the altar. I knelt at the communion rail. He prayed a simple prayer in English. It was direct and earnest. I said a silent prayer of my own: Dear God, thank you for sparing George's life. If it be thy will, let him live.

Chapter 5

SOON AFTER Father Fortin escorted me back to the surgery section of the hospital, the nurse brought her first report. "They've just begun surgery, Mrs. Wallace. The Governor's doing fine. We don't know about his liver yet."

"Is there anything special you would like for me to pray about?" Father Fortin asked me.

"Well, the doctors think his liver may be damaged," I said.

"Then we'll pray for his liver," he said, as he began to finger his rosary. And pray he did. Beads of perspiration formed on his forehead as he concentrated and spoke softly under his breath.

The nurse told me there was a call from Mrs. John Connally. "Do you want to take it?" she asked.

The Wallaces and the Connallys had a mutual admiration for each other. John Connally began his first term as Governor of Texas in 1962, the same year George Wallace was elected Governor of Alabama for the first time. When George and I attended our first White House dinner, Nellie Connally was George's dinner partner, and he enjoyed her company very much. Both men were Democrats during the Nixon administration, but lately there had been a great deal of speculation that John Connally might join the Republican Party.

"Yes, I'll speak with Mrs. Connally," I said. I knew George would want me to take the call.

"Cornelia, we're so upset over what happened to George," Nellie said. "We haven't been able to get any news about his condition, and I wanted to hear it from you. How is he?"

"He's going to be all right, Nellie. I just know he will."

"How are you holding up?"

"I'm fine, Nellie. Tell me, are you-all going to stay in the Democratic Party or are you going to join the Republicans?"

Nellie did not hesitate with her reply. "We're Democrats, of course. Tell George we called, and if we can do anything, let us know." A short time later John Connally announced that he was leaving the Democratic Party to become a Republican.

Nellie Connally's call was the first of several that were put through to me that evening. I've never yet been able to figure out how, with all the confusion, any calls got through at all that night.

Joanne Walker called from the Mansion. "How is George?" she asked.

"He's still in surgery. What about the children? Do they know?"

"Yes, they know, and they're taking it fine. We're arranging to get some of them up there. What about the little children? Do you want them to come?"

Joanne was referring to my two sons, nine-year-old Jim and eight-year-old Josh Snively, and eleven-year-old Lee, George's youngest daughter.

"No, I think it would be better not to upset them any more than necessary."

"What about Lee?"

"Maybe Lee should come. I'm afraid she might think her father is dead unless she sees him alive. She probably needs to be reassured more than the others."

"Cornelia, I feel as if you need someone to be with you. Do you want me to come up?"

"No, Joanne, I'll be all right—but, Joanne, if anything happens to George, get here in a hurry."

The first members of my family to reach me were my cousin Rachel Folsom Lichenstein, her husband, Bob, my cousin Linda Folsom Ottesen, and her husband, Henning.

Most of the Alabama congressional delegation came to the hospital and were admitted to the surgery section. There was no waiting room in that section, so some chairs were placed in the doctors' dressing room.

Senator Hubert Humphrey had arrived early. He was very comforting. He wrapped my hand over his arm and strolled up and down the corridor with me, all the time talking in a well-modulated tone. His words were consoling and his voice had a soothing effect on me. For the first time I felt calmer and less anxious.

People outside of political circles find it hard to understand how politicians can be rivals and at the same time maintain a friendly personal relationship. It does happen. Senator Humphrey had visited the Governor's Mansion in Montgomery the previous fall as a member of the Senate Agricultural Committee. He is a warm and tender man, a humanitarian in every sense of the word, and there is nothing phony about him. If he is guilty of one political sin it's that he cares more about people than politics. He struck up a warm relationship with our daughter Lee, and she returned his affection by calling him "Uncle Huber." Naturally, when her father and Senator Humphrey met head on in the Democratic primaries, Lee took her autographed picture of Uncle Huber off the wall and put it in a dresser drawer until after the campaign.

Senator George McGovern was in Kalamazoo, Michigan, campaigning. Although he canceled his schedule after the shooting, he was too far away to come to the hospital. Eleanor McGovern was at her home nearby when she heard of the shooting, so she came to represent her husband. Eleanor is tiny, pretty and charming, and I liked her very much. She and I had been on several television shows along with the wives of the other candidates. As we talked in the hospital corridor that evening, I knew that she realized it could have been her husband instead of mine.

When a political candidate is shot, it is an assault on the whole political system and, more dangerously, a threat to the democratic process. This was the feeling conveyed in the statements made by many prominent political figures:

Senator Edward Kennedy: "My heart and prayers go out to Governor Wallace and to members of his grief-stricken family. Once again, democracy in America has been scarred by senseless and unforgivable violence. I am saddened beyond measure that tragedy has again stained and darkened the process we use to select our political leaders."

Senator Hubert H. Humphrey: "Any act of violence adds to the tension in this country. What we need more than anything is a spirit of reconciliation."

Vice President Spiro Agnew: "Our concern goes out to the Governor's wife and children at this hour, as well as the families of others wounded in this brutal assault."

President Richard M. Nixon: "The shooting of Governor Wallace was a senseless and tragic incident. The nation has suffered more than enough already from the intrusion of violence into its political processes."

Lieutenant Governor Lester Maddox of Georgia: "The shooting of Governor Wallace was far more than the shooting of a man. Those responsible are guilty of shooting America. They are not the enemies of Governor Wallace, but enemies of America, enemies of the people and enemies of freedom."

Senator George McGovern: "We can only hope and pray for the speedy recovery of Governor Wallace, and we can only say a prayer for our country. If we've gotten to the point in this country where a public figure can't speak out on the issues of the day and seek the presidency without being shot, then I tremble for the future of our nation."

After two hours the nurse reported to me again: "Governor Wallace is doing fine. There is no damage to the liver."

Father Fortin's face was radiant as he heard her words. "Thank you, Father Fortin," I said.

"They're going to explore the chest cavity and whole abdominal region," she explained. "I'll keep you posted."

A few minutes later the operating-room doors swung open with a bursting force. A green-suited Jimmy Taylor staggered into the hall pulling off his face mask. He was as green around the gills as the scrub suit he was wearing. He braced himself against the wall and looked as if he might faint.

"What's the matter?"

"Nothing," he said unconvincingly.

"Are you all right?"

"I just had to get a little air."

Jimmy had been standing by George's side at the time of the shooting, which was more than enough trauma for one day, plus the fact that his shift had gone on duty at 8 A.M. Un-

"What would you do if you were First Lady?" Betty Hughes asks.
"Jane? . . . Cornelia? . . . Muriel? . . . Eleanor?"

Three of the joys of my life—
Josh, Lee and Jim—at the U.S. Capitol.

fortunately for Jimmy, there had been no time for replacements. Bill Breen, the agent who had pulled me away from George, was also in the operating room because there were two entrances and both had to be guarded. I later learned that Jimmy Taylor's hasty exit from the operating room was caused not only by the sight of blood or the need for air. He had just watched Dr. Schanno lift George's intestines and pile them on top of the patient's chest.

Billy Joe Camp told me that Captain Dothard had been released and asked if I would like to see him.

"Released? Already? How can that be possible?"

"He was treated for a flesh wound and the doctors released him," Billy Joe said. "He's just down the hall."

We left the surgery section the same way we entered it. Uniformed police officers were stationed at every door and at regular intervals along the corridor. We passed a young woman in street clothes. She must be a member of the hospital staff, I thought. No, she wasn't. She held a pencil and a legal pad in her hands. She had to be a reporter. How in the world did she get in that hallway? A few years ago I had heard a very unpleasant story about a journalist who covered Jacqueline Kennedy when she was hospitalized for the delivery of one of her children. As the story went, an ambitious young woman reporter climbed up a laundry chute to gain entry to the building. I say young because an older woman could not have accomplished the feat. I was simply appalled at the lack of consideration for the privacy of the Kennedy family. Now I had a feeling we were about to get a sampling of the same.

Families form strong bonds during times of crisis such as deaths, illness and injury, and they need their privacy. If they are alone with each other they will freely express their love, appreciation, emotional needs, strengths, weaknesses, dependency and hurt. An outsider's intrusion on the family's privacy during these trying times may inhibit or prevent this natural, healthy and needed expression of feelings.

As we walked to the other end of the corridor, we passed a set of double doors leading to the lobby. It was full of people. They were milling around everywhere, some talking, some walking, some just standing around. All were awaiting word of the fate of George Wallace. A small crowd had gathered outside the hospital. The actual words of the radio bulletin were: "George Wallace was critically gunned down today in a Laurel, Maryland, shopping center. He was taken to Holy Cross Hospital in Silver Spring, Maryland, where he is still undergoing surgery. There is, as yet, no official report on his condition."

People wanted to know what was happening and they came to the place where they thought they could find out. But there was no report on George's condition. The only people who could deliver that information were wearing rubber gloves and still had instruments in their hands. They were not concerned with the people's need to know; they were concerned with the life of the man on the table before them. They were concerned with the strain on the heart that pounded beneath the chest, with the blood that their patient had lost and was losing; they were concerned with the rhythm of the lungs as they pumped up and down. How much longer could they twist in and out of blood vessels and tissue, cutting and sewing? How much longer could their patient's body stand the shock? They did not know. Any surgery which lasts over two hours is risky, and for George it had been three. From this point on they would consider that fact seriously and repeatedly, because every minute they continued, George Wallace's life was on the line.

The people knew his life was in jeopardy, too, and they began to pray. In Birmingham, Alabama, people of all denominations filed into the football stadium at Legion Field to attend the Billy Graham Crusade. In 1968, Billy Graham had gone to Montgomery to offer his condolences to George after his wife, Lurleen, died. He had subtly suggested that George not become a presidential candidate in 1968. (There's an old saying down South about a preacher who gets involved in politics: "He's done quit preaching and gone to meddling!")

But Billy wasn't "politicking" that Monday evening in Birmingham. On the night before we left Maryland George had called Billy, promising him that we would attend the crusade on Thursday night. Now Billy was praying to God to spare the life of George Wallace. How ironic that Billy Graham should be in Alabama on this particular night. I believe in the power of prayer, and 50,000 people prayed for my husband at that service. I'm especially thankful to those people because George needed those prayers.

I had first met Billy Graham in 1959 in Sydney, Australia, when the Roy Acuff Show (with which I appeared) was filming a television series there. After our performance we all went to the Billy Graham Crusade, where Roy Acuff was invited to sing, but being the modest man he is, he declined. When the meeting was over, we were introduced to Billy Graham. I remember that his blue eyes had a very special quality. He was a handsome man, but it was something from inside that put the shine in his eyes. He impressed me then as being a very special person.

Billy Joe and I reached the end of the hall on our way to visit Dothard. We entered the last door on the right. Inside the room, to the left of the door, was a nurses' station. I saw three women behind the counter, but none of them wore nurses' uniforms. I assumed they must be hospital personnel. One of them was talking on the telephone and writing on a pad. Dothard, fully dressed, sat at a long conference table talking to two FBI men.

He didn't look like the man I had seen on the ground at Laurel. The color had returned to his face and he looked relaxed, although serious. His recovery seemed miraculous to me, which goes to show how inaccurate my visual diagnosis was. I was glad to see him up and it helped to have something to feel good about. We sat and talked. He showed me the bandage on his stomach and described the wound. The bullet had entered just above his waist at the right side of his midsection, traveled between two layers of skin and exited on the left side. In all probability he would have received a more penetrating wound except that the bullet had hit George first. His was called a flesh wound, which means it won't kill you but it smarts. (I don't know why, in the movies, they always say it's "just" a flesh wound!)

Dothard told me that his wife was already en route to Maryland. He asked about George, and I told him all I could, which was not much more than saying he was still in surgery. Satisfied with Dothard's condition, I stood up to leave when I noticed that the woman with the phone in her hand at the nurses' station was no longer behind the desk. She had stretched the coil wire of the receiver all the way out to its full length, trying to get closer to where we were. She had been eavesdropping on the FBI interrogation.

No one seemed to notice her unusual behavior until I pointed her out to the Secret Service agent. "That woman's a reporter. I saw her earlier, writing in a notebook."

The agent looked at me as if I were crazy.

"I tell you, that woman's a reporter," I said emphatically.

The agent approached the woman and said, "I'll take that phone." She refused and moved out of his reach. He repeated his statement twice, each time in a stronger tone, and twice she moved away. Then he grabbed for the phone and she kicked him. Finally the agent put his arm around her waist, picked her up and walked out the door. The last I saw of her going out the door, she still had the phone in her hand.

Several weeks later the same agent came to me and asked me for a deposition. The woman was a reporter and had sued, accusing him of assault. I gladly obliged and added that I would be more than happy to testify in court. The case was dropped.

The hospital had a new crisis on its hands. Billy Joe Camp had been juggling the press as well as he could. The hospital public-relations man tried to help but this catastrophe was out of hand. He didn't seem to understand a politician's obligation to his public. Even when he's dying? you ask. Yes, especially when he's dying. George had been in surgery over three hours and the press still had no news of his condition. I guess they forgot doctors don't take a coffee break when they're elbow deep in a human body. If the doctors were not available, they wanted to hear from Mrs. Wallace.

"There are three hundred members of the writing press out there, Mrs. Wallace," Billy Joe told me. "They want you to come and say just a few words to them."

"I can't. I just can't face that many people right now."

"Mrs. Wallace, they just want to hear some word about how the Governor's doing."

"I know, but I can't do it. All the questions they'd ask and you know how persistent they can be. I couldn't stand being subjected to the pressure." I was still harboring some resentment about how most of the writing press had distorted George's image.

"Mrs. Wallace, I assure you they won't be unkind at a time like this."

"But can you guarantee it?"

"No, ma'am."

"I didn't think so."

Billy Joe wouldn't give up. "There are people all over America watching their television sets, waiting for a report on the Governor's condition," he said.

I knew what he meant. "I don't want them to go to bed thinking he's dying. I *know* he's going to live. Tomorrow is Election Day, and people just won't vote for a dying man." I really had no choice. "I don't want him to be cheated out of those votes." I refused to see the writing press but I agreed to go on television. "The only people I'll see are David Dick, CBS; Rebecca Bell, NBC; and Steve Bell, ABC."

Billy Joe argued for one pool member of the writing press. I still refused. "I'll go set it up," he said.

One of George's political appointees had overheard my discussion with Billy Joe, and while I was sitting in the make-shift office talking to the congressmen from Alabama, this well-meaning but not politically astute friend came and told me he didn't think I should go on television. The more he talked, the more I realized that he believed George was going to die. It was obvious he had no faith. His attitude was one of half mourning already, and the more he tried to bury George the madder I got. His negative thinking made me furious. First, I hadn't asked for his advice, and secondly, I resented his telling me what to do about my husband. I was married to one of the most famous political figures in America and I came from a political family a mile long. In fact, I must have absorbed my political instincts in my mother's womb because the whole time she was carrying me she was campaigning for her brother, who was running for governor. I didn't ask for those instincts; I didn't want them. I just happened to have them. And this man had never even run for public office!

Also, I felt he was questioning whether I was rational or overcome with emotion, which I resented even more. The more he protested, the more antagonized I became. I felt at a time like this I shouldn't have to argue with anyone. Then he implied that my reason for going on television was purely politically motivated. That was not true but he seemed to forget—alive or dead, George was first, last and always a politician. He didn't realize how it would boost George's spirits after this ordeal if he won Maryland and Michigan, and how much his spirits would need that boost. Did he understand how it might upset George and throw him into a state of depression if he lost those two primaries? If he didn't know that, he didn't even know George as well as Dr. Schanno did, because that was to be the strategy Dr. Schanno would employ to boost George's morale three days later and would continue to use—the political challenge as a means of getting his patient to fight back during the rest of his hospitalization.

Alabama Congressman Bill Nichols and his wife, Carolyn, encouraged me to make the television appearance. They, too, believed that George would make it. They had gained faith through a similar experience. Bill had been injured in the war, paralyzed in one leg, and the other leg had to be amputated at the knee. Now he walked with an artificial leg. (I had noticed a brace on his shoe when we attended Mendel Rivers's funeral, but I thought he had been a victim of polio and only needed slight support.) He had been in hospital beds, flat on his back, for years and was told he might never walk again, but he was determined to walk and he did. His wife also believed that he would walk and she encouraged him not to give up his struggle. Bill was elected to Congress after he successfully conquered his handicap. That night in the hospital he told me how he still experiences nerve pain in the end of his leg, and hearing that, I had a rebirth of appreciation for all the times he had met George and me at the airport when we came to Washington. I remember only one trip when Bill sent a staff person and that was because he was out of town.

The faith and courage of those two dear people inspired me.

"George will make it," Bill assured me. "He's got determination."

"Don't let him give up, Cornelia," Carolyn said. "You can

help him when he's down. Make him keep going, even when he doesn't want to."

Bobbie Jo, George, Jr., Peggy Sue and Lee had arrived. Bobbie was the oldest, and for a few years after her mother's death she had filled a maternal role for the younger children. Now she had a husband and three-year-old son of her own. She was clutching a handkerchief and her eyes were red from crying. George, Jr., looked dejected. His head was slightly bowed as if to hide from the world the hurt his eyes might reveal if someone looked into them. Lee was nervous. She didn't seem to be able to grasp the situation completely and although I could tell she had been crying, she was doing much better than I had expected.

Peggy Sue was the most distraught of all. When I put my arms around her, her body convulsed with sobs. "I talked so ugly to Daddy this morning," she said, choking on her tears. "He asked me to give him my paper and I told him to get his own paper; I'll never forgive myself! Why was I so mean to him?"

Peggy had naturally blown the argument out of proportion. Taking both her arms I pushed her away from me so that I could look straight into her face. "Because you're a child, Peggy. The way you behaved this morning is the way any normal girl your age would have behaved. You have no reason to feel guilty about what happened between you and your father this morning. Now don't let me see you feeling sorry for yourself again."

The Wallace children were victims of tragic circumstances. They had lost their mother four years ago after her year-long battle with cancer when Bobbie Jo was twenty-three, George, Jr., sixteen, Peggy Sue eighteen and Lee only seven. Immediately their father plunged headlong into the 1968 presidential primaries and campaigned from May until November. Although George took the children along on many of his trips and came home every weekend, he was not with them enough to offer them the emotional support they required. They, in fact, carried the burden of emotional support for him. With the letdown of defeat and the slump of inactivity after the 1968 campaign, George fell into a delayed state of mourning. When I came into his life he was experiencing long periods of depression. He sat in his house for days on end and would only go out occasionally, in spite of constant urging from his friends.

I know the children's faith in God must have been a little shaken. I know they must have wondered why, if God loved them, he had let them suffer so much pain. Now they had been dealt another cruel blow. When they left Alabama they only knew what the rest of the world knew: Their father had been shot and his condition was critical. They did not know about the paralysis because no word had left the surgery section of the hospital about it.

I took them into the doctors' lounge. When they were seated, I told them. "One of the bullets hit your father in the spine. He's paralyzed."

There was a new outbreak of tears, my own included.

Later in the evening my mother and my brother, Charles, arrived. As always, when I needed them, my family was at my side.

The bullet in George's spine was not a life-threatening situation. No matter how terrible the paralysis, it was not given top priority. The life-and-death problem was always the massive wound in the stomach area, and the longest part of the surgery involved repairing the damage to the stomach and intestines and cleaning up the food spillage in the abdominal cavity. The doctors elected to save George's life first and deal with the bullet in the spine later—it would not matter whether he walked if he wasn't going to live. The University of Maryland team of doctors, which Governor Mandel had summoned at my request, arrived sometime after the surgery was begun. They were satisfied that the Holy Cross surgeons had things well under control, but they remained at the hospital scrubbed and ready as a backup team and also to consult with the other surgeons, particularly about the bullet in the spine. Dr. Hamilton Hutchinson and Dr. Garber Galbraith arrived from Alabama in time to join in the consultations.

After five hours, the exhausted Holy Cross doctors completed their work on George's abdomen. They turned George on his side and inserted a large needle into the base of his spine. Dye was injected and pictures were taken at different stages of the procedure to determine the exact location and position of the bullet and to be sure it was not blocking the flow of the spinal fluid.

I was waiting in the doctors' lounge when the three neurosurgeons, Drs. Baltazar Perez, James G. Arnold and Garber Galbraith, came in. Everyone else was asked to leave the room.

"We have placed dye in your husband's spinal canal," they explained. "There is a missile located at the lumbar-one level inside the spinal canal. The bullet is not blocking the flow of spinal fluid. The paralysis he has now, we feel, was immediate, and will remain unchanged with the removal of the missile. Your husband has undergone five hours of surgery and it is our unanimous conclusion that to submit him to further surgery at this time would greatly endanger his life."

There was never any question in my mind about the doctors' decision to delay the removal of the bullet in George's spine.

After the neurosurgeons gave their report, Dr. Schanno gave me a brief summary of George's condition. He had a superficial wound on his right forearm and a superficial wound on his right upper arm. Both were clean and there was no bone damage. There was a flesh wound at shoulder level in front and a deep grazing wound above his right shoulder blade. One bullet had entered his stomach, traveled around and lodged in the left flank. Another entered between his sixth and seventh ribs and lodged in the spinal canal.

His colon was nicked but not perforated, which was extremely fortunate. Perforation of the colon would have caused severe infection from the spillage of the bowel contents.

"There's one thing," Dr. Schanno said, frowning. "All the food in the stomach was blown and scattered into all areas of the abdominal cavity. We scrubbed the cavity and removed the blood and food particles as best we could, but in all probability he will have abscesses from food contamination. There were no solid pieces of food to remove. It was nearly impossible to remove all the tiny particles. I'm sorry but there's not much we can do about that. One good thing we can tell you: We examined your husband's blood vessels and found no traces of cholesterol or fatty deposits, no hardening of the arteries. Your husband has the cardiovascular system of a twenty-year-old man. He's a remarkably healthy individual. I would almost be willing to guarantee that he will never have a heart attack."

Dr. Schanno told me that George would be taken back to the recovery room and I would be able to see him in a few minutes.

"By the way, Mrs. Wallace, do you mind telling me what your husband had to eat?"

"Chopped sirloin steak," I replied.

The hospital PR man, Tom Brandon, had told Billy Joe earlier that the hospital staff could no longer cope with the three hundred members of the news media. In an attempt to ease the situation he had moved the press to a new location outside the hospital. That meant that if I wanted to go on television I would have to leave the hospital. Not wanting to be separated from George, I refused to leave. Billy Joe asked for a compromise, but Tom Brandon was afraid that if he gave an inch he would lose a mile. Billy Joe finally wangled a crew to man the lone television camera that had been abandoned when the news media representatives were moved to another location.

There were millions of people who were still awake that night who were afraid George was dying, and I wanted to relieve their anxiety and reassure them. I knew that millions of negative thoughts could not help George get well, and I wanted the people of this country to share my faith that George would live. I felt that the people would not necessarily believe a group of strange doctors if they said George would make it. But I knew if I, his wife, could stand before millions of people under such trying circumstances, composed and confident, and tell them George was all right, they would know I was telling the truth.

I did not rehearse any words or write them down. I did not plan what I would say. For a minute I was afraid I might forget the names of our children, but I didn't worry about the rest, because I knew that God would give me the strength to say what I needed to say and supply me with the proper words.

With the children accompanying me, I went before the camera. "I would like to make this one brief statement," I began. "I just want to tell you, myself, that my husband is in very

62

good condition. The children and I are going in to speak to him in a moment. Before he went into surgery he was conscious all the time and quite aware of everything that was happening to him. He was talking to me all the time from the accident to the hospital. I feel very optimistic about him. You know his nature. He didn't get the title of the Fighting Little Judge for nothing. I'm very happy and I feel good that he is alive, that he has a sound heart and a sound brain and all of his vital organs are solid. I can't thank God enough for that."

I purposely did not mention the paralysis because I could not explain the aspects of it. There were too many things I didn't know. I decided to leave that for the physicians, who would issue a complete medical report as soon as possible.

I'm not sure what effect my brief television appearance had since by morning all the news services would be carrying the story that George had survived. The children and I returned to our makeshift waiting room on the first floor. A short while later a nurse told us that George was in the recovery room, and we could go in to see him.

George was draped with a sheet, and white gauze encompassed his chest. Attached to his left arm was a tube leading to a bottle containing intravenous fluids. He was still groggy from the anesthesia but responsive. I leaned over and kissed him on the forehead. "You did fine, darling. You're going to be all right."

Each of the children greeted him and offered him words of encouragement. Too sedated to converse, he smiled softly and winked.

It was now around midnight, and no full report on George's medical condition had been released since he had been shot at 3:58 P.M. The press had been moved to the Boys Club about a block away from the hospital, which is where the attending physicians held their first press conference about an hour later. Dr. Schanno was elected spokesman by his peers, and it was a good choice. Billy Joe coached him for his first session, instructing him to tell the truth about George's condition. In case he got pushed too far he gave him a phrase to fall back on: "I don't care to comment on that at this time." Although he admitted to being nervous, Dr. Schanno did a superb job, and as he continued his role as "mouth man" for the medics he became more relaxed and confident. He even began to enjoy it.

The general line of questioning that night was "How badly is the Governor hurt?" "Will he ever walk again?" "Will he still be a candidate?" Dr. Schanno stuck to his guns. He was candid and truthful but he honestly did not know whether or not George would ever walk. Some of the press interpreted his failure to satisfy their answers as evasiveness. A few suspected that he was withholding pertinent information which if revealed would indicate George was close to death. The questions began to take on severely pessimistic overtones and some could only be answered with a negative prognosis of George's health. It was obvious that part of the press was preparing to write George's obituary.

Billy Joe Camp conducted all the press conferences. Since I chose to stay at the hospital with George, I wanted to have some idea of how the conferences were going and I wanted to hear it from two points of view, so I asked Bob Lichenstein to attend each session with Billy Joe. Billy Joe and Bob briefed me after each session. At one point they told me they were not altogether pleased with the way the press was responding to the facts they were being given.

I wanted to feel the pulse of the press because I knew that what they wrote would affect the people who read it. While I wanted the people to know the truth, I didn't want an unnecessarily dark picture painted. The truth was dark enough without any twist of the pen in that direction, but it was far from dismal.

Now Billy Joe and Bob were beginning to see some of the stories coming out of the press conference. Some of the columnists had written seemingly factual stories about things of which no one, not even the doctors, had knowledge. Some reporters were deliberately embellishing Dr. Schanno's statements to the point of pure sensationalism. Soon we were getting feedback from the stories, and the implication was that George Wallace was not doing as well as his doctors would have people believe. Rumors were rampant that George was a dying man.

As we discussed methods by which we could convince people that George was not dying, it seemed that only one would suffice. We would allow the press to see for themselves; we would agree to have George photographed in his hospital room. Billy Joe was ready to call a pool photographer; then we decided we should use David Cloud, our own personal photographer, instead. That way we could select the best picture and not take a chance on the press releasing a bad photograph. I suggested to Billy Joe that we wait until we had the results of the Michigan and Maryland primaries and then photograph George with the victory headlines. The picture would not only show George Wallace's political triumph but would also show him triumphant over death.

George remained in the recovery room for an hour before he was transferred to an intensive care unit on the seventh floor. A room was made available for me three doors away from the intensive care unit so that I could be near him. Outside his window overlooking the front grounds of Holy Cross Hospital, hundreds of people still kept their vigil. In Houston, Texas, the local ministers made public announcements that the doors would remain open for people who wished to pray for the critically injured Governor of Alabama.

The attending physicians reported George's condition as critical, and the next three days and nights were crucial. The ground rules for visitors were laid out immediately: I was allowed to be at his bedside at all times; the children and other close members of the family could visit for fifteen minutes, according to the hospital's standard I.C.U. procedures; no other visitors were allowed. If there was some friend especially close to George who might boost his morale, I could discuss the possibility of a visit with Dr. Schanno and he would consider it. I was in complete agreement with the arrangement.

This was my first experience with Dr. Schanno's gutsy manner, and I liked the way he took full control and responsibility for his patient. He was not in the least affected or intimidated by the fact that his patient was a famous man. He had good political bearing and did not hesitate to use his innate common sense. Not only was he a brilliant cardiovascular surgeon capable of the most delicate surgery, but he was also a very fine artist, who later presented us with several watercolor landscapes that we treasure only second to his surgical work on George's body. Although he possessed all the talents and attributes of a creative artist, he did not play the prima donna. He was good-natured and optimistic, decisive, conservative and somewhat homespun. He was a short, feisty little man—a great sportsman and knee deep in family life. In fact he was much like his patient, the Fighting Little Judge.

Dr. Herman Magazini, by contrast, was quiet, serious and very sensitive. His eyes seemed to mirror the sadness of the whole world, and in his deep black pupils I seemed to read his compassionate longing to correct the hurts of mankind. And if he couldn't correct the wrongs of the world, at least he seemed to say, I understand your suffering, whatever it may be.

Chapter 6

THE DAYS AND NIGHTS all seemed the same. During those first three crucial days I did not sleep or eat. My concern for my husband was so great that it replaced all my physical needs. I didn't drink coffee to stay awake and I didn't take tranquilizers to calm me down. I had no artificial props, only the one real sustaining Power. I believe anyone could stay awake three days and nights, but I don't believe it possible to do this, as I did, without being tired and exhausted except by the grace of God.

George slept most of the time because he was administered large doses of medicine for pain. I finally learned the timetable for his injections and scheduled my visits to coincide with his waking moments. If he had a shot he would usually sleep soundly for two to four hours, so I would return to his room at about the time I estimated the medicine would wear off. If he awoke in between, the nurses would call me from my room down the hall and I would stay with him until he fell asleep again. During the entire time I stayed at the hospital I wore street clothes, since I usually went into George's room every two hours during the night. I would bathe and put on a fresh dress once a day. Even later, when I began to sleep a little during the day or night, I still never wore a gown or robe for fear George might need me at some unexpected moment. I was on call every minute day and night.

The nurses were superb. They turned George from one side to the other every two hours to keep him from getting pneumonia, and if the bed sheets became wet from perspiration, they changed them. They were diligent in their duties, much to the doctor's delight and their patient's chagrin. Once, when I went into George's room he was scowling. "These nurses are such eager beavers!" he said. "Can't you get them to leave me alone so that I can sleep?"

Tuesday, May 16, was primary day in Maryland and Michigan. On the six o'clock news, reporters interviewed some of the people going to and from the polls, asking them, "Did the shooting of Governor Wallace affect the way you voted?" All of them said no. Some said they prayed for his recovery but did not indicate how they had cast their ballots. I was not able to determine any trend in the voting from the news. Reporters later quoted one of the staunch Wallace supporters in the Michigan campaign headquarters as saying, "I'd have voted for George Wallace if he was dead." Another said, "He'd make a better president dead than any of those others alive." Obviously, there were many supporters and nonsupporters who still were not sure whether the bantam Governor of Alabama would live or die.

Later that night Billy Joe brought the official word on the outcome of the two state primaries. Happily, I relayed the message to George: "Darling, you won both primaries!"

He smiled faintly, then looked somewhat astonished. "Both primaries? I won Michigan *and* Maryland!"

Although he was very weak, George managed a big smile.

On Wednesday, May 17, the *Baltimore Sun* carried this headline: WALLACE WINS MICHIGAN AND MARYLAND. Because George had been so heavily sedated the night before, I was afraid he might not remember that I had told him about his victory or he might think he had dreamed it. Billy Joe and I decided to show him the paper. Billy Joe added a word of caution: "Unless you think this picture might upset him."

I looked at the front page where Billy Joe was pointing his finger. Right below the bold black type was a picture of a youngish-looking man who appeared to have close-cut, light-colored hair and wore glasses. There was nothing unusual about him except the weird grin on his face—a strange, sick sort of smile. The caption under the picture read: "Arthur Bremer being held in the shooting of George Wallace." I had learned sometime during the long hours of surgery that a white male had been taken into custody at the scene of the shooting. I had heard that, if the police had not carried him away, the crowd at the rally probably would have killed him. Governor Mandel had informed me that the man was not a resident of Maryland. I was glad to know that.

But now, for the first time, I was seeing the face of the man who had tried to kill my husband. The face was unfamiliar to me. I couldn't relate to it. As I stared at the photograph I felt no hate, no antagonism, no malice, no bitterness, nothing. I had not seen the person who held the gun and pulled the trigger. Neither had George. Arthur Bremer would forever remain an abstract figure to us. Except for the reports we heard and read about him, he was completely foreign to us, both then and now.

Not knowing how George would react to seeing a picture of the person who shot him, and at the same time wanting very much to boost his morale by showing him the headlines, I elected to show him the paper but not the photograph. With a pair of scissors borrowed from the nurses' station, I carefully cut out the picture of Arthur Bremer from the middle of the front page. The print from the second page filled the empty square and I counted on the state of George's weakened condition to blur the print so that it would seem to be all on the same page.

Newspaper in hand, I walked triumphantly into George's room. "Look, darling!" I said, offering him the paper.

Feeling much better than the night before, he took the paper and studied it.

"Read it, read it!" I said, pointing to the lead story.

As he scanned the headlines his face beamed. "Tell Billy Joe to get the official vote count."

George was so pleased with his victory that he consented to be photographed holding the newspaper in his hospital bed. It was to be the first picture of him to be published since he had been shot only two days before. Even the pain and discomfort he

was experiencing could not dim the gleam of his joy and satisfaction.

No one could ever know what winning those two primaries
meant to my husband. He was amazed at his own accomplishment and grateful to the people who voted for him. He has
cited that achievement more than any other single feat as a
means of restoring his confidence and self-esteem during his
recovery and to this day. What happened to my husband was a
horrible thing. He almost lost his life, he lost the use of both
legs, but if he had lost two political elections on top of that and
all within a few days of each other, it would have been a total
disaster for him. I believe it would have been almost impossible,
under those circumstances, to supply him with sufficient moti-
vation to overcome his illness and his paralysis.

From his sickbed in a Maryland hospital, George had
maintained his political stature in the Democratic Party. Adding the Michigan and Maryland victories to his Florida, North
Carolina and Tennessee wins and his second-place standings in
the Pennsylvania, Indiana, West Virginia and Wisconsin primaries up to that date put George one and a half million popular votes ahead of his nearest opponent. That was enough
political power to keep his desires fired. The Democratic National Convention would be the goal—the sunrise over a dark
mountain. He was certainly in the shadow of death and he
would have to lift himself out of the valley with a lot of help
from all of us. He certainly couldn't walk out.

On the third day after George was shot, his waking periods
became longer. Dr. Schanno allowed us to install a phone in
his room so that he could call his mother, who had recently
undergone brain surgery and was not able to travel to Maryland. I felt that some contact between mother and son would
be beneficial and reassuring to both of them.

Dr. Schanno removed George's name from the critical list
that same day. When he discovered that his patient enjoyed
watching television he ordered a set installed in his room.
Hee Haw was the show George wanted to see most of all, and
I sat in his room watching it with him, hoping the light, folksy
humor would cheer him.

George had not been able to brush his teeth, although the

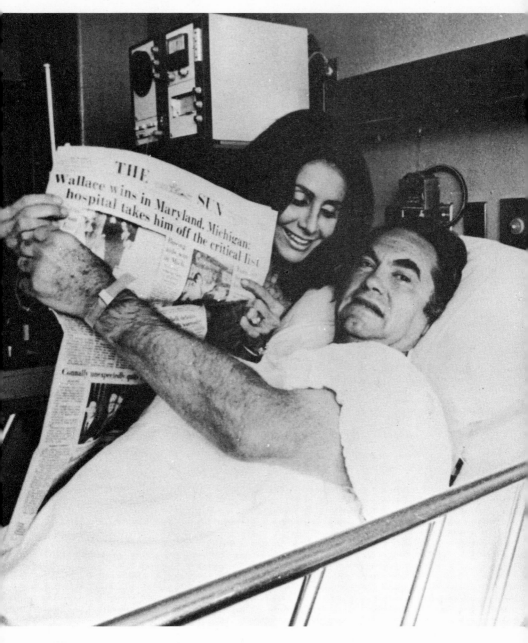

Showing George the victory headlines in Holy Cross Hospital.

nurses regularly cleaned his teeth with toothpaste-flavored sponge sticks. However, it wasn't the usual vigorous brushing to which he was accustomed. Like all good politicians he was very conscious of "bad breath" and it bothered him that he could not practice good oral hygiene. Every time I leaned over to kiss him he would turn his head, offer me his cheek and say, "I've got bad breath." One night we were watching *Hee Haw* when right in the middle of the show Junior Samples popped out of the cornstalks and said, "Bad breath is better than no breath at all!" George and I had a good laugh and he never again refused me a kiss or complained about his bad breath.

George knew he had been shot in the spine as soon as he was hit by the bullets. While he lay sprawled on the ground he realized he couldn't move his legs. Even in the hospital emergency room, George diagnosed his own paralysis before a team of physicians was able to do so accurately. Yet no one had actually told him he was paralyzed. The doctors had not orally confirmed his diagnosis that afternoon in the emergency room, and he had no knowledge of the conclusion reached by the neurosurgeons when they examined him following surgery. Sooner or later, however, he would ask someone about his condition, and I suspected that someone would be me. I dreaded hearing those words, but I knew they were bound to come. What would I say? Sick as he was from his injuries, it seemed too cruel to make him face the possibility that he might be crippled for the rest of his life.

It came just as I had anticipated. Without any warning, about three days after he had been shot, George looked at me earnestly and asked, "What about my legs?"

"Well, what about them?"

"Am I going to be paralyzed?"

"We don't know for sure. We'll have to wait and see."

"I can't believe this has happened to me," he said. "I'm shot all to pieces and I'm paralyzed."

"George, you're alive—and that's all that matters."

"But I can't walk."

"You can wake up every morning and see your toes, and there are some people who can't do that."

72

"What am I going to do?"

"You're going to keep on doing what you've always done. Fortunately, you don't make your living with your legs. You make your living with your mind and your mouth, and your future doesn't depend on your walking around. Except for the inconvenience of getting from one place to another, your life doesn't have to be any different."

I wasn't getting through to him. "Why has this happened to me?" he said. "If I were a mean man, maybe I could understand it, but I've never done anything to hurt anybody. I didn't deserve this."

I said, "This is a heck of a way to get elected President."

George looked puzzled. He was not fully aware of the outpouring of sympathy he was receiving. I tried to explain.

"George, I now this may be hard for you to accept, but perhaps this is part of God's plan for you. There were many people who hated you and who refused to listen to anything you had to say. When you opened your mouth they automatically closed their ears and minds. No one will hate you now. Everyone will be sympathetic. When you talk they'll listen. For the first time in your life you have the ears of the world open to you. You have an opportunity to make yourself heard. The hatred has been erased by your suffering. If God allowed his own Son to suffer the agony of the cross, surely you can endure this burden."

"This may be more of a burden than I can bear. I am not sure I'm that strong."

I tried to help him make some sense out of what had happened to him. "George, maybe God is testing you. I know it's easy for me to say that, because I'm not the one who is paralyzed, but perhaps you're looking at it in the wrong light. Why don't you try to look at it as one more challenge? This is nothing unusual for you. You've had to struggle all your life. When you were eighteen and your father died, you had to struggle to get through college. When you were in the Air Force and had spinal meningitis, you had to struggle to live. Then, after you became Governor, you had to struggle to overcome the death of your wife. George, maybe God is giving you the greatest challenge of your life—and you'll triumph over this tragedy just as you did all the others!"

"What am I going to do about the campaign?"

"What do you want to do? Are you ready to throw in the towel?"

"No, I'm not ready to throw in the towel, but I can't run a campaign from a wheelchair."

"Well, Franklin Roosevelt did. Are you any less a man than he was?"

"No, I'm no less a man. If he did it, then I can, too."

The Roosevelt image seemed to give George something to live up to, and yet the parallel between the lives of Franklin and Eleanor and George and Cornelia does not go further than these two points: the wheelchair and politics. I did not become George's legs, and George did not use me as a substitute to make his speeches. I felt my talents would be put to better use if I gave George emotional support and helped him get well so that he could do his job himself.

On Thursday I went to visit Secret Service Agent Nick Zarvos, whose condition was critical. Although we were not aware of it till some hours later, Nick had been shot in the neck and had been whisked away in a car as he vomited and held his throat, trying to stop the blood that was squirting through his fingers. He had almost been killed trying to keep my husband alive, and I wanted to express my gratitude to him in person. Since it was impossible for George to visit Nick, I was also bearing a message of appreciation to him from the Governor.

Agent Zarvos was in Walter Reed Hospital in Bethesda, Maryland, a short drive away. Much to my astonishment, when I started my departure from Holy Cross, three Secret Service agents immediately flanked me. Because there were so many Democratic candidates entered in the 1972 presidential primaries it was virtually impossible for the Secret Service to extend protection to the candidates' wives, and I had not had any personal security during the whole campaign.

The Secret Service began protection on March 19, 1972, after the Florida primary had weeded out five of twelve Democratic contenders. Agents were ordered to cover Edmund Muskie, Hubert Humphrey, George McGovern, Henry Jackson and George Wallace, at a cost of $1 million a month. The candidates

74

were told that the agents were assigned solely for their protection and that coverage did not extend to family or staff.

The Secret Service had increased its numbers three times since the 1968 presidential campaign because the agents had been so overworked. Some of the men had quit the force, and some stayed on only to have their wives quit *them*.

I had always traveled with my husband, so I did not feel the need for a bodyguard. There were always agents around and, although I knew they were assigned to George, I didn't doubt that someone would come to my assistance if the need arose. There was one day, however, during the Wisconsin primary when I did have some doubts about that. George was rushing to an early morning TV taping in Milwaukee. We were running late, so when our car stopped at the curb George (who clipped off a quick pace when he wasn't in a hurry) and all the agents went flying into the building, leaving me still struggling to get out of the back seat of the car. The sight of those six strong men running after one man and the thought of me, abandoned on a cold, isolated street in a strange city, momentarily filled me with disgust. I could picture how the scene would look on the six o'clock news—not too good for the candidate's image. I wasn't being treated like a lady, so why should I act like one? I climbed out of the car and with all the force my five-foot-six-inch frame could muster, I raised my hefty foot, planted it firmly against the open car door and slammed it shut, hoping for all the world that one of the television networks had recorded it on film. I could imagine it being shown with a subtitle—How Not to Treat Your Wife When You Campaign—and George watching and squirming as he learned his lesson. Injury was almost added to insult when, in a valiant effort to catch up, I scampered after the last agent entering the building and caught the backswing of a two-inch-thick glass door. My little mad spell melted in five seconds, and I quickly forgave the agents for their unchivalrous behavior as I appreciated how seriously they considered their job of protecting my husband's life. When I issued report cards the next day, I gave all the agents a big D for Discipline—and George a fat F for Forgetting he had a wife.

The only time I felt the need for security for myself was

while we were campaigning in Wisconsin. I asked for an off-duty agent, specifically requesting one who was born and raised in the North and could snow-ski. The children had flown up for the weekend and I had promised them a day of skiing. They had never seen snow and I had never skied, except on water. I selected a ski slope from a Wisconsin map full of resorts and made my plans to fulfill my promise to the children. I asked for the agent, not to protect me from some unknown assailant but, I hoped, to keep me from breaking my neck. There was, however, no agent available to accompany us. Thanks to Jack Paulsen and Grey Hodges, two members of our campaign staff, we had a very successful trip. The children skied like champs and I came back without any broken bones and also without my dignity, having left it in the snow and slush at the bottom of that hill I never conquered.

When I had needed an agent the most, my request had been denied, but now, when I hadn't even asked for one, I had three agents to escort me to visit Nick Zarvos.

"Gee, fellows, how did I rate this?" I asked.

"We were issued a new directive after your husband was shot," Agent Jim LeGette replied. "You and all of your children will be under Secret Service protection at all times when you are in the Washington, D.C., vicinity."

"That's nice," I said, "but I'd prefer to think I don't need you."

"We hope you don't," Jim said. "But we'll be around if you do."

We exited through the basement level of the building, and as we passed a storage room a long-haired figure emerged from the door. I froze in my tracks and started shaking like a leaf until I saw that the figure was a young janitor pushing his broom. I was definitely experiencing trauma from the shooting.

When we reached the automobile I felt safe and calm. As we pulled out of the parking space the agent reached for the radio to notify the Command Post of our departure.

"This is Agent LeGette," he said. "We have—" He put the microphone to his chest. "Mrs. Wallace, we don't have a code name for you. What would you like to be called?"

"Ripcord Two, of course," I said with a smile, not believing I could really use Ripcord, the code name for the Governor.

"We have Ripcord Two departing Holy Cross Hospital en route to Walter Reed Hospital."

When we arrived at Walter Reed Hospital, Nick's wife and mother were at his side. Looking at Nick's wife, I felt a strange surge of guilt because she and her family were forced to suffer this agony as a result of my husband's misfortune. Perhaps she thought of it as an occupational hazard, accepting the danger as part of her husband's job, but I found it very hard to justify the fact that another man was severely wounded when my husband was the intended victim.

Nick's face was swollen twice its normal size. He was bandaged all about the head and the neck, and he still had a tracheotomy tube. He looked tired but pleased to see me, and before I could say anything more than "Hello" he motioned for his pencil and pad and began scribbling a message: *How is the Governor?*

I was touched by his concern for the man he had tried so diligently to protect from harm. "He's fine. He told me to tell you to hurry and get well so you can go to Miami to the convention with him."

Nick smiled.

Nick's wife walked down the hall with me when I left. I asked if there was anything we could do for her or the family, but the President and the Federal Government had already taken care of their needs. The President also had offered Nick his choice of assignments, specifically suggesting the coveted Key Biscayne or San Clemente posts.

Eventually Nick's injury would require additional surgery. The tracheotomy incision would be closed, but the bullet that had barely missed his jugular vein and shattered his jaw also had damaged his vocal cords. There was some doubt as to whether Nick would ever talk again, and if he did, his voice would never sound the same as it had before he was injured.

Later in the day a member of the White House staff called to ask whether the Governor was well enough to receive a visit from the President on Friday. Dr. Schanno welcomed the idea, as he thought it would be good therapy for his patient.

On the day George was shot President and Mrs. Nixon appeared on television offering their "hopes and prayers" for the Governor's recovery. The following day the President walked across the White House lawn to shake hands with a crowd of people who had gathered outside the fence. After what had happened to George, I found it appalling that he would unnecessarily expose himself to a group of strangers. In retrospect I suppose that public demonstration was the President's attempt to restore confidence and quiet the fears of a nation badly shaken by the attempted assassination of George Wallace. I'm also confident that the President's hospital visit was devoid of political intent and that its sole purpose was to offer encouragement to the victim of a tragic episode in American history.

Dr. Schanno informed George and me of the President's impending visit and the appointed hour. For security reasons the visit was to be kept secret from everyone else. Early Friday morning the nurses simply were told to prepare the Governor for a very important guest. The nurses gave their patient a fresh shave, splashed some good-smelling after-shave cologne on his face, changed his sheets, tidied up his room and even managed to dab a little powder and lipstick on their own faces.

At 8 A.M. the Secret Service agents began clearing the floor, and patients were told to remain in their rooms with the doors closed. No one was to be in the halls. Suddenly I realized that I had a problem on my hands. One of my best friends, Marilyn Fillingim, had come up from Atlanta to boost my morale and now I didn't know what to do with her. I knew she was too energetic to stay in one place for five minutes unless I "canned" her. Feeling bound by the secrecy oath, I offered Marilyn no explanation as I firmly led her by the arm, put her in my room and instructed her not to dare move until I came back for her. She was dumbstruck but she complied. That was the only time in all the years I had known her that I had ever seen her with her mouth closed.

The Secret Service was monitoring the movements of the President. He had been at Camp David, Maryland, going over some papers before his upcoming trip to Moscow. Then he helicoptered to Walter Reed Hospital, where he visited Nick Zarvos, and left by car for Holy Cross. Just before 9 A.M. an agent advised us that the President was five minutes away.

The announcement was like a shot of adrenaline to George. "How do I look?" he asked.

"Fit as a fiddle," I told him.

"Is my hair combed right?"

"Yes, but I'm sure the President won't be looking at your hair."

In his usual thoughtful way, George invited his nurse to stay and meet the President. Dr. Schanno and Sister Helen Marie Auth, the hospital administrator, also waited in the room with us. They were like two children waiting for Santa Claus, so eager to exhibit their prize patient—and rightfully so, since his survival was a testament to the superior medical facility they staffed.

The President arrived with very little commotion. I greeted him at the door, Dr. Schanno and Sister Helen Marie welcomed him on behalf of the hospital and George introduced his nurse. The President responded in the same affable manner as when I had met him twice before, but which he rarely was able to project to his television audiences.

The first time I had met President Nixon—in May, 1971, in Mobile—I was concerned because his skin had a grayish tone. My uncle, who had recently had open-heart surgery, had the same gray look before his operation, which made me suspect President Nixon might have heart trouble or at least a circulatory problem. I didn't mention my concern to anyone out of my own sense of national security. However, when I heard someone remark that the President "looked like a warmed-over corpse" during his trip to Mobile, I was convinced that he was not in perfect health. On the day he came to visit George he was wearing television makeup, and I wondered if it was strictly for the camera.

"Mr. President, you're mighty kind to take the time to come see me," George said.

"You look as if you had a good night's sleep," the President replied.

"They don't let me sleep much. They have to turn me every two hours."

"Governor, you look so well, you would think you were in here for a tonsillectomy."

"These doctors and nurses are the best."

"I can see they're taking excellent care of you, but I want to extend once more the use of the Presidential Suite at Walter Reed Hospital. It's available to you if you care to use it. My staff will make the necessary arrangements should you decide to transfer there."

"You're mighty kind, Mr. President, but if I get well enough to leave here, I'd like to go back to Alabama."

"That's certainly understandable."

The President thought his trip to Moscow might interest George and he promised to send General Alexander Haig, deputy assistant to the President for national security affairs, to the hospital for some briefing sessions after he returned.

As the President left George's room he turned to me and said, "The Governor looks remarkably well, considering all he's been through. He's alert and in good spirits."

"Yes, sir, the doctors are amazed at his recovery," I said.

"From what I hear, you've been good for the Governor. He has the determination to overcome this thing."

"Yes, sir, I know he will," I said confidently, and added with a smile, "We expect to be out there running against you in November."

The President offered a jovial retort: "I certainly wouldn't want to run against *you*."

By the time the President reached the corridor people had lined up along the walls outside the intensive care unit. Feeling guilty about the shabby way I had treated my friend Marilyn, I asked the President if I might introduce him to my guest. He graciously consented and I retrieved Marilyn from her isolation. She was probably the only person in the hospital who was surprised to see the President of the United States, and I concluded that I must have been the only one who kept his visit a secret.

The President was the first of many dignitaries who came to pay their respects. In the days that followed, Lawrence O'Brien, Chairman of the Democratic Party, visited, which was significant because heretofore the Democratic Party leaders had virtually ignored George's candidacy. Mainly because of his maverick third-party efforts in 1968, the Democratic Party loyalists had been hesitant to welcome him back into the fold, and George had made political hay out of their opposition. Emphasizing in his campaign speeches the fact that he had been shunned, he raised a sympathetic cry from his followers.

In the midst of the 1972 presidential primaries, the Democratic bigwigs of Detroit decided to sponsor a huge fund-raising dinner for the party. They chose the time of the traditional Jefferson–Jackson Day to throw a big gala banquet. It was built up to be the biggest hoopla ever held, aside from the national convention. Since the Michigan Democratic primary was not far off, the party officials in that state decided to invite all of the leading Democratic presidential contenders—all save one, George Wallace.

George Wallace was amused by the insult. Cagey, crafty and the hero of countless political battles, he formulated his plan of action. True to his gutsy, aggressive style he decided not to retreat but to meet his opponents in a head-on dinner. He would stage a Jefferson–Jackson Day celebration of his own. Party loyalists had reserved Cobo Hall with 20,000 seats. Instead, George Wallace would rent the fairgrounds on the same night with a 20,000-plus capacity. Instead of the $100-a-plate admission, his dinner would be free, and the only things he planned to serve on his menu were his verbally chopped-up Democratic opponents with a dash of Louisiana hot sauce and Alabama hot pepper relish. Wallace served it up himself. He dished it out and his crowd ate it up and asked for a second helping.

George was a nervous wreck all the way to the fairgrounds that night. He knew if his people didn't turn out he would have political mudpie all over his face. As we approached the fairgrounds, the traffic became so thick we were barely able to proceed.

"It looks as if you're going to have a full house," I said.

"Honey, don't be silly, these people are going to the fair," George said. "You think everybody in the world loves me the way you do."

We inched along so slowly that it took us thirty minutes to reach the fairgrounds from the main road, and when our lane of traffic finally came to a standstill, our driver pulled out and drove down the left side of the road.

"George, you'd better plan to make two speeches," I suggested.

"No, I'm not going to make two speeches!"

We were almost an hour late getting into the hall, and George was afraid that the crowd might have dissipated before we arrived. His fears were unfounded. Greyhound buses were lined two deep and mounted police were trying to manage the crowd. When we entered the building it was jammed and overflowing. There were people in the aisles, lining the walls, pushing up against the platform in front, and some were trying to squeeze in the doors in the back. Pleased as punch, George lit right into his tirade.

"I knew it! I just knew it, but I can hardly believe it!" I said to a member of the road crew.

"Mrs. Wallace, you ain't seen nothing yet," he said. "Come with me." He took me out the door we had entered and all the way around to the other side of the building, where there were more people and more people and more people.

"Mrs. Wallace, the Governor's gonna have to make two speeches," he said.

"Well, *you* tell him. Maybe he'll believe y'all."

When George finished his speech, he removed his coat and there wasn't a dry thread in his shirt. Some of the boys bent his ear for a moment and George conceded. The hall was emptied and filled to overflowing again, and George gave his second speech with the same gusto he had exhibited in the first. He had drawn 20,000 people to his Jefferson–Jackson Day celebration while the party loyalists across town were able to muster only a small gathering of 3,000.

On the editorial page of one of the newspapers I chanced to see a column titled, "Politics Is the Best Tonic for George Wallace." That man was certainly right. Dr. Schanno was in full agreement with the amateur physician and he gave his patient a spoonful of political tonic whenever he thought it was needed. He allowed politicians to visit even when he denied friends. I knew the therapy was good for George but it was also an embarrassing situation.

"It's terrible," I apologized to everyone. "All of his enemies can get in but none of his friends."

Senator and Mrs. Edward Kennedy came to the hospital. So did Ethel Kennedy. There was no mention of politics. Senator Kennedy related his own recuperative experience after surviving a plane crash in which twenty-five of his vertebrae were fractured. I greatly appreciated the encouragement and counsel he gave George.

Ethel Kennedy was every bit as charming and vivacious as she is portrayed in print, but I was a little surprised that the contours of her very feminine frame were not emphasized in the stories I had read about her. Tanned and natural, she managed to look healthy despite the cast on her foot and the crutches she still used. Knowing her plaster trophy was awarded for her efforts on the ski slopes enhanced rather than diminished her sportsy appeal.

Congresswoman Shirley Chisholm was among the many political dignitaries who came to the bedside of the stricken Alabamian. Of all his political opponents Shirley Chisholm was the only one Governor Wallace had not publicly attacked. He did not omit her name from his onslaught of criticisms because she was a woman or because he considered it politically expedient. As George put it, "She says the same thing in Florida that she says in New York." At the same time he chastised the other Democratic presidential candidates for changing their stands on issues "as many times as they changed their underwear."

Although Mrs. Chisholm and George took different stands on many political issues, there was one stand they took together in George's room that day: their faith in prayer. The Congresswoman held George's hand and as she placed her other hand on his forehead she bowed her head and prayed for the restoration of his ailing body. When she said good-bye to George his brown eyes glistened with tears, and observers who witnessed the Congresswoman's departure from the hospital reported that she, too, was crying.

Chapter 7

THE HOLY CROSS PHYSICIANS confirmed George's paralysis during their first press conference but they did not offer a definite opinion as to whether the paralysis was temporary or permanent. Medically, it was impossible for them to draw positive conclusions as to the degree of walking ability George would have until they examined the injury to the spinal cord at the site of impact. There were several possibilities: (a) if the spinal cord was bruised he would regain normal use of his legs, (b) if the cord was slightly damaged he could regain partial use of his legs, (c) if the damage was severe he might regain little or no use of his legs and (d) if the cord was completely severed he would be permanently paralyzed.

While we waited for the bullet to be removed from George's back we hoped and watched for signs that would indicate the damage was slight. Ultimately, time would tell the true story.

Shortly before eleven thirty one night, Elvin Stanton, George's assistant press secretary, urgently sought me out in the confines of the seventh floor. He was visibly shaken.

"Mrs. Wallace, I've just learned from a network correspondent that the *Washington Post* is right now setting its type to run a headline tomorrow which will read WALLACE'S SPINAL CORD SEVERED," Elvin said.

"Severed? But that's not true. His spinal cord is *not* severed," I replied.

The only way anyone would ever know would be to open

the spinal canal and take a look. The surgery on George's back had not been performed. So how could the *Washington Post* say George's spinal cord was severed when even his doctors did not know?

"At twelve A.M. that press will roll with the headline. We've still got time to stop the story but we'll need someone who can offer proof that it's not true," said Elvin.

"We can ask the neurosurgeon, Dr. Perez," I suggested.

"We'll have to do better than that. We'll have to get a statement from him," he said.

Elvin dialed the number for the Perez home. He awakened Dr. Perez from a sound sleep but the doctor was unperturbed and happy to accommodate us by issuing an official statement of denial as the neurosurgeon in charge of the case. Elvin wrote on a pad as he talked to Dr. Perez.

When Elvin hung up the phone I turned to him and said, "Can you imagine how this will affect George if he picks up a paper and reads that his spinal cord is severed? The shock and hurt will be too much for him to bear. It'll fill his mind with doubts. He'll probably never believe the truth if he ever reads that story."

"You're right, psychologically it could have a very damaging effect on the Governor," he said.

"Elvin, you've got to stop that headline!" I said. "Call the paper! No, call the editor! You call the owner of that paper and threaten to sue if you have to, but get that story stopped!"

Elvin called the paper and reached the night editor. He identified himself as one of Governor Wallace's press secretaries. The man believed Elvin was legitimate but he wouldn't buy Elvin's side of the story. Elvin read the statement from Dr. Perez and gave him the neurosurgeon's private telephone number, adding that the doctor was immediately available to answer any questions. "We're asking you to retract the story," said Elvin.

"I'm sorry but we received our information from a reliable source and we're going to run the story as is," said the night editor.

Elvin came back with a final word. "I told them the story was false, but they are going to print it anyhow."

"Even if it were true, they shouldn't print that story. A man shouldn't have to wake up and read a thing like that in the newspaper before he hears it from his doctor. Well, I guess we'll just have to wait and see. Maybe they'll have a change of heart and decide not to run it," I said.

The papers hit the street at 4 A.M., but we didn't wait. We sent a staff member to the Washington Post building. On top of the stack was the glaring headline, WALLACE'S SPINAL CORD SEVERED. Late in the morning I took George his daily papers, all save one, the *Washington Post*. He noticed the paper was not among those I handed him.

"Honey, they forgot to bring me the *Washington Post*."

"No, they didn't forget to bring the *Washington Post*," I said.

"Well, where is it?" George asked.

Looking straight at him, I did one thing I never do to my husband. I fabricated a story.

"They're all sold out," I said.

George, Jr., was making a late visit with his father one night when out of curiosity he tickled the bottom of his dad's foot. The senior Wallace's toes wiggled. In disbelief the son pulled back the sheet and asked his father to watch as he repeated the procedure. Young George rushed to my room in excitement and beckoned me to come substantiate what he had discovered. We hurried back to the intensive care unit and I watched as once again George, Jr., stroked his father's foot. The toes moved separately and distinctly.

George, Jr., and I stared at each other in astonishment. Unable to contain our jubilation we called in the night duty nurse to share our discovery. This was the sign we had hoped for—some indication that there was still some nerve life in those limbs. There was no doubt George's toes had moved. But there was some doubt whether the movement could be taken as a sign George would ever be able to walk again.

When Dr. Schanno made his rounds the next morning we were waiting for him. Dr. John Haberlin, who had assisted that first night in surgery, was with him. Together they listened intently as we related the events that had transpired during the night. I don't think they doubted our word but I do believe they suspected what we had seen was only an isolated incident.

Eager to verify or dispute our claim the doctors quickly initiated their own examination.

"Let's take a look," Dr. Schanno said. He took a door key from his pocket and scraped it firmly from the bottom of George's heel up the center of his left foot; then he scraped it up the center of the right foot in the same manner. All ten toes wiggled. He repeated this procedure several times with the same positive results. He turned to Dr. Haberlin.

"John, he definitely has movement in his toes. I'm not sure what it means, but I think it is involuntary movement."

Dr. Haberlin, who was not ready to concur with his colleague, proceeded with his own examination. Without offering any physical stimulus to the Governor's feet, Dr. Haberlin said, "Governor, let me see you move your toes."

The toes moved in response to Dr. Haberlin's oral command. Dr. Haberlin repeated the command and the toes obeyed without physical stimulus again. The third time he issued the order and once more the toes nodded in answer.

"Joe, in my opinion that's voluntary movement," Dr. Haberlin said.

Dr. Schanno was not sure. "Governor, you definitely have some movement in your toes. Dr. Haberlin and I cannot agree whether it's voluntary or involuntary movement."

I think Dr. Schanno would have preferred not to make public notice of his findings because the movement could not be accurately interpreted at that time. However, the members of the press gained knowledge of the discovery almost immediately. Later we learned that one of the nurses working the intensive care unit had a close personal relationship, through her husband, with a member of the press corps, and we attributed this and many other press leaks to her "loose lips."

When confronted with the knowledge of the fact by a newspaperman, Dr. Schanno was forced to make this public announcement at the next press conference:

"The Governor exhibits normal reflex action when the sole of his foot is stimulated. Both feet evidence movement but the movement is more pronounced in the left foot. The significance of this involuntary muscular activity in relationship to the final degree of recovery from the paralysis is difficult to ascertain at this time but it is most encouraging."

However, after the disagreement between Doctors Schanno and Haberlin as to whether George's toes had moved voluntarily or involuntarily, medical tests were performed in an effort to make a more scientific diagnosis as to how much actual damage George's spinal cord had sustained. Dr. James Duke, chief of the physiotherapy department at Holy Cross, was summoned to conduct a series of tests with an electromyograph. The instrument is designed to measure and record muscular contractions. Long needles were placed deeply into the muscles of George's legs; the needles were then connected by wires to a sensitive machine which measured the electrical activity in the muscles much like an electrocardiograph or electroencephalograph. The test, in effect, should show whether the nerves supplying energy to the muscles have been interrupted.

The first test was administered on June 2 while George was still in the intensive care unit. With my husband's kind permission and in an attempt to present as clearly as possible the medical condition regarding George's paralysis, I will quote in toto from the medical charts the results of these tests:

ELECTROMYOGRAM   I.C.U.   June 2, 1972
Physician: Dr. James Duke   Patient: George Wallace

Abnormal EMG: On the basis of slight denervation activity of diffuse distribution and encompassing the myotomes of L2 through S2. *Summation:* EMG study of both lower extremities was carried out with samplings of the myotomes of L2 through S2. On each side the same muscle groups were studied. Scattered denervation was present in both lower extremities and was considered to be minimal in degree. Denervation consisted of predominantly positive sharp waves with occasional fibrillation potentials found in isolated areas of the various muscle groups studied.

In most areas sampled no denervation was present. There appeared to be somewhat greater denervation in the quadricep muscle bilaterally than in any other muscle groups studied. In no instance was the denervation persistent.

Motor units under voluntary control were not demonstrated in any of the muscles studied.

A motor nerve conduction study was carried out for the left common peroneal nerve between the knee and ankle. The conduction velocity over this segment was well within the normal range.

IMPRESSION [by Dr. Duke]:

Full development of EMG abnormalities in peripheral nerve disorders usually requires approximately three weeks from time of injury or onset. This study was done at eighteen days following injury and in general we would expect to see most of the electo-diagnostic abnormalities by this time. The explanation for the relatively slight denervation cannot be clearly determined at the moment. It would appear that there are two possible explanations however:

1. Insufficient time for development of full denervation, or

2. Relatively slight damage or injury to the lower motor neuron system.

Serial EMG studies in the near future should help to clarify this uncertainty.

The second test was carried out one day before the surgery was performed to remove the bullet from George's spine.

ELECTROMYOGRAM   ROOM 716   June 17, 1972
Physician: Dr. James Duke   Patient: George Wallace

Abnormal EMG: Severe and essentially total in degree involving all myotomes of both lower extremities in a neuropathic fashion. *Summation:* EMG studies of both lower extremities was carried out with samplings of the myotomes of L2 through S2. Definite changes are noted on this examination comparison to the earlier study. Today I found rather profuse denervation quite readily in all areas sampled in contrast to the initial examination in which only very minimal and spotty denervation was present. The denervation today consisted of numerous fibrillation and positive sharp wave potentials in practically all areas sampled. The degree of denervation seemed to be greatest in the quadricep muscles bilaterally.

No evidence of voluntary motor units activity was detected.

A motor nerve conduction study was again carried out for the common peroneal nerve between the knee and ankle. This was within normal range and essentially unchanged from the initial examination.

My own personal conclusion from studying the results of these tests is that none of the movements of the toes were physical evidence that George would regain any ability to walk but that these were simply common phenomena associated with paraplegia.

There were other occasions after we left Holy Cross and returned to Montgomery that elevated my expectations that George might walk again. One of those incidents occurred several months later at the Mansion. George was in the midst of his morning personal hygiene routine when suddenly his right leg rose up in the air straight out in front of him. His leg remained completely suspended without support for a full fifteen minutes. I can't begin to tell you how excited I was since the only insurmountable problem to get a paraplegic to stand is for the knee to remain rigid while the body is in a full vertical position. As a lay person, upon seeing his leg in this stiffened position, I immediately interpreted this as proof that his legs did have enough life in them to support the weight of his body. I was thrilled at the prospect.

When the physical therapist, Gary Buck, arrived an hour later to supervise George's exercise program, I joyfully revealed to him my discovery of the morning. I indicated to him that I strongly suspected that George had some latent ability to use his legs (incorporating this stiff knee). Gary Buck had come to us from Ranchos Los Amigos, a famous rehabilitation center in California. Being the well-trained therapist he is, Gary accurately described the stiff-leg syndrome as a result of severe muscle spasms experienced by most of the paraplegics with whom he had worked and observed.

It would be difficult to express in words the disillusionment I felt over learning that the muscle spasms I had seen could not be transferred to any practical functional use for George's legs. It was disheartening to once again have to face the prospect that George might never walk again.

I can recall many times in the months that followed after we returned home when George would be asleep at night and I would sit up in the bed next to him watching endlessly as the muscles in his legs twitched and contracted with a regular rising rhythm. Although by that time I had learned that these, too, were muscle spasms I hoped with every ounce of faith in my soul that I was witnessing the slow deliberate process of God's miraculous healing power.

Sometime on or about the second anniversary of George's "accident," as I like to call it, Dr. Garber Galbraith, George's neurosurgeon from Alabama, was attending a meeting of the American Medical Association. When he was queried about the possibility of George's walking again Dr. Galbraith made this statement: "With the passing of time the possibility of Governor Wallace ever regaining the full use of his legs becomes more unlikely."

In all honesty, by the time Dr. Galbraith made his statement, George and I both were fairly reconciled to the fact that George would probably be paralyzed for the rest of his life. We had exhausted all hope of finding any conventional medical cure but we still had faith in God and we still believed in miracles.

Chapter 8

GEORGE REMAINED in the intensive care unit located on the top floor in the northwest corner of the hospital for several weeks. It was accessible by only two doors. The door connecting the coronary care unit had been sealed; the other one was still in use. He was kept there for security as well as medical reasons.

The bullet was still in George's spine and it had to come out. His doctors planned to remove it as soon as he was able to undergo another operation. George was doing so well that we were contemplating moving him back to Alabama, where the surgery could be performed by Dr. Galbraith, who was Chief of Neurosurgery at the University of Alabama and had operated on my uncle, Governor Jim Folsom, and George's mother, Mozelle.

There was one other aspect over which we all agonized. The Alabama Constitution stipulates that

> if for any reason the Governor shall remain outside the boundaries of the state for twenty days, he from that day has no official capacity to act until he reenters the state boundaries, whereupon he automatically is restored to his full authority. On the twentieth day the Lieutenant Governor shall assume the duties of the Governor and act with full power, without any financial compensation.

The prospect of George Wallace losing his governorship—even temporarily—seemed more than he could bear psychologically. We were fearful that it would retard his general recovery. When the doctors were made aware of the constitutional time-table, they heartily agreed that it was in the best interest of their patient to return him to Alabama as soon as possible.

There was much speculation in the news media that George would be moved to Walter Reed Hospital for the surgery. We encouraged that rumor simply as a red herring to ensure George's safety so that when we made the move to Alabama we could do it without making him vulnerable to a second attack. When I went to see Nick Zarvos at Walter Reed, I deliberately made my visit obvious. Before I left I even toured part of the hospital and talked to some of the doctors on the staff.

Holy Cross Hospital had been receiving an average of three bomb threats a day, the first soon after George arrived. As a matter of fact, one day there were so many bomb threats that when the hospital switchboard operator rang the Secret Service Command Post room and told an agent she had a bomb threat on the line, he said, "I'm sorry, we've taken as many bomb threats as we can today. Tell them to call back tomorrow."

He wasn't being frivolous. It just happened to be the end of a long day and everybody was beginning to get tired from the hospital routine. Here was a group of healthy, energetic people who for months had been on and off airplanes, in and out of cars, packing and unpacking luggage every night and every morning, struggling through crowds of people two or three times a day and once every night, then—wham. They were stopped still without a "cool down."

When you train fine horses or athletes, you always walk them out to cool them down after a good workout. The system requires it. Our people didn't have that opportunity, and it was a depressing sight to see our staff lose that quick, efficient pace and sink into the doldrums day by day. It was like the sadness you feel when the circus folds its tents and pulls up its stakes to move on to another town. All the anticipation and high expectations were fading.

Our staff people had been riding with a winner and they liked it. They took pride in the fact that they were helping put George on top, so they worked hard long hours. If they were tired, they laughed, and if they were sick they didn't complain. I've always said, "Politics is the king of sports," and we had a winning team, only our quarterback was benched and would have to sit out the rest of the game.

One night as I left George sleeping in his room, I stopped to pass a few words with Agent Breen, who had tried to pull me away from George at Laurel. "This is quite a change of pace, isn't it?" I said. "I know it must be a difficult adjustment for all of you to sit around a hospital for so long."

"We don't mind, Mrs. Wallace," he said. "That's our job, and we just want the Governor to get well. By the way, we all had to turn in a statement of the incidents we witnessed at the shooting, and I had to file a report on your actions."

I was curious. "What did you report about me?"

He studied me a moment, as if he were not quite sure how I would react. "I told them you were either the bravest woman I have ever met or a fool," he said.

I was amused. "I don't know if I'm the bravest woman you've ever met, but I'm certainly no fool," I said. "I'd appreciate it if you would amend your statement to that effect."

Several days later the agent informed me that his statement now read: "The lady is not a fool."

This was the first time I had any indication that anyone had questioned the motives behind my actions that day, since I consider it perfectly natural for any woman to protect her loved ones when they are in danger.

The plans to move George to Alabama were being stepped up. The Secret Service took full charge of the necessary arrangements. They advised me that no one would be told of the exact time of the move and that everything would be handled with the utmost secrecy.

Unexpectedly one night an agent came to my room and told me to have all my extra luggage packed and ready to be picked up at 3 A.M. He instructed me to keep only what I could fit into one suitcase and carry in my hand. I had a steam iron and some other odd-shaped articles that would not fit in any of my suitcases. Out of my desperate need, I sent a highly trained physician on an errand to bring me a cardboard box from the basement supply room. It was almost 3 A.M. when I stuffed the last object in the box, taped it up and put a cord around it. I started to write my name on the box so it wouldn't get misplaced when I suddenly realized I couldn't. If I didn't put my name on the box the bomb squad would undoubtedly open it and check it. I'd never get everything back in that box if it was emptied. On the other hand, if I *did* put my name on the box it would be a ready target for sabotage. What a predicament. This may seem like an insignificant event, but because of the uniqueness of my husband's situation this box had become a big problem for me.

I stared at the box helplessly. It didn't even bother to stare back. It just let out its little subdued papermill odor and sat there. I had an idea! I would use the code name assigned to George by the Secret Service. I grabbed a black crayon and in bold letters I wrote on the box: RIPCORD II.

All our meticulous plans were foiled. George had an abscess. The suite especially prepared for George and me at the University of Alabama Hospital would go unused by us. George would lose his governorship and Lieutenant Governor Jere Beasley would assume the office. I would not go home to my three small precious children who were not yet out of school for the summer, and George would not, at this time, return to his beloved Alabama soil.

Because I could not go home to the children, Lee, Jim and Josh came up from Montgomery for the weekend. I missed them and I hoped their visit would lift George's spirits. The abscess made him feel bad and his stomach was so swollen it seemed to be "three feet high and rising." The bandages on his incision added another two inches to his ballooning midsection. When the children came in the room and saw how mountainous he looked under the white sheet, Josh asked, "Are you going to have a baby?"

The food particles from his intestines had finally done their dreaded dirty work. A bulge as large as a grapefruit emerged on his left side and his abdominal area was distended, causing him much discomfort. His temperature soared. The abscess would have to be drained.

Dr. Schanno decided not to return his patient to the operating room but instead elected to carry out the surgical procedure in the intensive care room. Using a local anesthetic and a surgical knife, he made an X-type incision in the center of the swollen area. Enough pus to fill a fruit jar gushed from the opening. After Dr. Schanno had opened and drained the abscess on the side, fresh pus began to ooze from the incision in George's stomach.

George was to undergo surgery two more times for abscesses after he returned to Alabama, but both times he would be given a general anesthetic. Although the general public was never aware of it, these abscesses caused him far more anxiety than any other aspect of his illness. They were the setbacks that discouraged him. Each time a pocket was discovered, his physical therapy had to be discontinued and then started all over again.

Until the drainage from George's midsection stopped it was impossible to open the spinal canal to remove the bullet because there was a danger that the infection might contaminate the spinal fluid. If that ever happened, the spinal fluid would carry the infection directly to the brain. The operation, therefore, was delayed.

George was so sick and weak from the abscesses that he became almost unresponsive. Once, as I stood by his bed, he looked up and said, "If it were not for you and my children, I wouldn't want to live."

One night he pulled my head down close to his and in a frail voice whispered, "I'm not going to make it. Tell Ralph I need to see him."

Ralph Adams had been a true and trusted friend since George had run Ralph's boardinghouse at the University of Alabama. I was always glad when George sought his counsel because I respected his judgment, but now I was disturbed by George's request. Ralph was also a lawyer, and it seemed obvious that George would look to him as the executor of his estate or perhaps for some final instruction about taking care of his dependents. I was convinced that Ralph was being summoned to hear the last requests of a dying man.

Ralph was in Alabama, but when I reached him by phone and explained the sudden change in George's condition and the urgency of his plea, he agreed to come immediately.

Hours later, when Ralph arrived, a much-improved George had recovered from his semidelirious state. "Hello, Adams," he said, "What are you doing here?"

"I came because you sent for me, Governor," Ralph answered.

"Well, what did I want with you?" George asked.

"I don't know," Ralph said, "I thought maybe you could tell me." Ralph stayed at the hospital for a day or so but his friend never remembered why he sent for him, so Ralph went home.

The telephone calls, mail and telegrams were pouring in. George received 300,000 pieces of mail at Holy Cross Hospital and we finally sent eighteen bags to Alabama, where each one was acknowledged. Get-well cards made up the bulk of the mail but there were many telegrams.

Among the telegrams were messages from Bob Hope, Billy Graham, Kathleen Kennedy, Anita Bryant, Lyndon Johnson and Sammy Davis, Jr. There was even one from the Vatican. The message was sent by an emissary to Pope Paul VI. I read each one to him, and some he asked me to read twice. With each one, tears came to his eyes.

George had always loved to read his mail. At home he asked for his mail before lunch and his meal always got cold as he read through the letters. When he was at work, once a day he would jump up from his desk, descend the staircase to the mailroom and thumb through the mail. He would read a few of the hand-penned notes while he was in the basement and then take a stack to pore over later in his office.

In the early days of our marriage, when George used to come home from the Capitol tense and strained from the rigors of the governorship, I would offer to massage his back to help him relax and unwind. He would refuse and ask for a foot massage instead. It was a private thing we shared and one from which he derived much pleasure. Now, watching him as he lay flat on his back in the intensive care unit, it saddened me to realize that never again would he be able to enjoy that simple pleasure—nor would I ever be able to provide that comfort for him.

This memory was especially painful when I went into

George's room one night as one of the nurses was finishing up her duties. She was the same nurse who had horrified me by winking at George while she was adjusting his I.V. drip only two days after he was shot. Each drop must be counted and I doubted her count could be accurate with her attention so diverted. She seemed more interested in impressing her patient with her charm than with quality nursing.

Whenever I came into the room to visit with George, the other nurses left us alone, but on this particular evening this young lady did not leave. She kept finding unnecessary little jobs about the room. I thought she was going to launch into a full-scale window-washing job. It was obvious she had no intention of leaving. It was equally evident she had no real purpose for staying. I decided I would outstay her as I felt I was due the consideration of a little time alone with my husband and, besides, I needed it. As she moved around the room, George followed her with his eyes. Finally she opened a drawer of the chest near his bed and took out a bottle of lotion. As I sat, staring, she pulled up the bottom of the top sheet and folded it back, exposing George's limp, crippled feet. Squeezing the lotion into the palm of her hand, she slowly began to rub it over one foot. Suddenly all my pent-up emotions seized me, and every nerve in my body felt as taut as the strings of a violin. I made a feeble attempt to converse with George, but he was uninterested. I felt unneeded, unwanted, more like an intruder than a wife. I seized an opportunity to reverse the roles and get the nurse out of the room.

"I'll do that," I said as I stood up and walked toward the foot of the bed to receive the bottle of lotion she would be forced to give up.

"No, let her do it," George said firmly.

That broke the string. I ran from the room to hide the tears that were streaming down my face. In my own room I fell across the bed, sobbing hysterically. It was the first time I had really cried since I realized George was paralyzed—I was due a good one.

Dr. Schanno had another problem to consider. George had begun to experience grabbing pains in his sides, and his ability

98

to tolerate the discomfort was considerably less with each awakening. Dr. Schanno prescribed Librium, varying the doses and watching George's reaction closely. He noticed that George experienced less pain while watching television, reading or conversing, so he reduced the dosage to a minimum and spaced out the time for administering the medication. He had to find out if his patient could get along as well on more guts and less medicine. Several times, when a nurse would come to him, I heard him refuse to change the orders on the chart, and one day when I ran into him in the hall outside George's room, he shook his finger in the air—a gesture much like the one George uses during his speeches—and informed me in no uncertain terms, "I'm taking him off that stuff. I don't care if he screams and yells all day!"

"Yes, sir!" I replied. "You go right ahead and do it. I have no objections. I'll even clap my hands and whistle 'Dixie.' "

By the fourteenth of June the grabbing pains in George's flanks became so severe that his doctors initiated an investigation to determine the cause. On June 15 an X ray made of the spine revealed some obstruction in the area of the bullet so that the spinal fluid was only partially flowing past the point. The bullet must come out. Dr. Schanno assessed his patient's condition: temperature was normal, drainage from the incisions on the flank and midsection had subsided. It was safe to proceed.

I arranged to have the children return to Maryland. Josh, Jim and Lee had gone back to Alabama to finish the last few days of school. George, Jr., had been making appearances for his father, trying to keep a spark of fire in the Wallace campaign. Bobbie Jo had the responsibility of her husband and little boy in Birmingham. Peggy Sue had gone home to Montgomery for a while to finish up her school term. After this trip Peggy stayed with me day and night through all the long weeks of her father's hospitalizations. She put aside all her personal interests and devoted herself exclusively to her father's recovery.

Now all the children again made the pilgrimage to Holy Cross Hospital. Early Saturday evening they gathered in George's room to celebrate Father's Day, and later that same evening George was prepared for surgery.

On the morning of June 18, Sister Helen Marie Auth, the hospital administrator, entered George's room and stood at his bedside. Instead of the familiar nun's habit, she wore a crisp white uniform, a stiffly starched white cap and her graduate pin from nursing school. She had decided to nurse the Governor herself. She was the model by whom all the other nurses set their standards. The hospital staff was elated over her change of roles, for although Sister Helen Marie was an excellent administrator, they knew her first love was nursing.

When the attendants came for George, Sister Helen Marie accompanied him to the operating room. Dr. Stacy Rollins, Dr. Garber Galbraith, Dr. Joseph Schanno, Dr. Guy Gargous and Dr. Hamilton H. Hutchinson, George's personal physician, comprised the operating team. They were scrubbed and waiting when George was wheeled in. When the patient was anesthetized, Dr. Rollins proceeded with the surgery. He made a six-inch-long incision in George's back, then entered the spinal canal at the level of the first lumbar vertebra. The bullet, surrounded by a large number of adhesions and encased in small nerve roots, was clearly visible. Dr. Rollins delicately teased away the adhesions and allowed them to retract into the spinal fluid. With a pair of small surgical forceps he gently extracted the lead bullet from the sensitive nerves. Mission accomplished! A graft patch of skin was inserted, the incision was closed, the patient was sent to recovery.

Within three hours George was returned to his room, where Sister Helen Marie continued to nurse him throughout the day. Watching her, I understood why she was so admired as a nurse and as a person.

Before the surgery there were diverse opinions about exactly how and when the bullet should be removed from George's back. Even the most qualified medical experts could not have made that decision without all the facts of the case at hand, and only the attending physicians possessed that information. Some critics have said that the bullet should have been removed the first night. To them I say, "I'd rather have a live husband with a bullet in his back than a dead husband with no bullet." If George had died in surgery, those same critics probably would have said, "The bullet should *not* have been removed." There are others who have said that the bullet should have been removed *sooner*. But they didn't know about the infection that racked his body for weeks. To them I say, "Gutrot." That's what George had, and a good case of it, too.

As to *how* the bullet should be removed, there were many unsolicited solutions offered by persons genuinely interested in the state of George's health. Eager to assist in his recovery, they did not sit idly by and criticize the treatment he was receiving, but instead devised highly imaginative methods for removing the bullet. One resourceful fellow sent a homemade "bullet removal kit" complete with instructions and guaranteed to get results or the merchandise could be returned. Guess what it was! A giant horseshoe magnet! The idea was to draw the bullet out (along with all the fillings in George's teeth, no doubt!).

A very ingenious technique was offered by another kind person who suggested that George take a simulated space ride so that while he was spinning in the gyro, strapped to his seat, the bullet would "sling out." (Everybody duck!)

There was also a lot of back-fence gossip about the bullet in George's back, and one rumor found its way into print. I can't remember the newspaper or the content of the story, but I'll never forget the headline: "Mrs. Wallace Makes Decision to Leave Bullet in Spine." I was taken aback by this revelation since I could not recall the doctors even *asking* my opinion and I was certain they were too intelligent to have taken my unqualified advice even if I had offered it. Doubting my memory of the conversation that had transpired in the consultation room that first night, I seized the paper and ran to Dr. Schanno.

"Did I do that?" I demanded, flinging the paper down on the table in front of him.

He read the paper, looked amused and said, "Of course not." When I continued my interrogation, Dr. Schanno gave me a serious answer, realizing that I needed reassurance. "No, you had absolutely nothing to do with it. It was purely a medical decision."

I was interested in the bullet in George's back from an investigative point of view as I was unsure as to the probability of conspiracy. I had been allowed to study the X rays with one of the doctors, and while there were signs of a shattered vertebra edge at the point of the bullet's entry, the vertebrae themselves showed no signs of fracture. From reviewing the film the doctor could only conclude that the bullet had entered the spinal canal through the soft tissue at the level of the twelfth thoracic vertebra and then dropped to the first-lumbar level. The doctor, who had virtually no knowledge of ballistics, was surprised when I pointed out that the bullet seemed to be resting in an upright position. However, I was more interested in the trajectory of the bullet than its final position because I was trying to determine how many bullets had hit George and from which direction they had been fired.

According to the audio on the CBS film and the lab reports on the weapon, there were five bullets fired from the would-be assassin's gun. But four people were hit, with six points of entry on George's body alone, as follows:

1. A bullet hole through George's right forearm (no bullet found)

2. A bullet hole through George's right upper arm (no bullet found)

3. A wound in George's right abdomen, with bullet located in flank

4. A bullet hole through George's right rib cage, with bullet located in spine

5. A bullet hole through George's right front shoulder (no bullet found)

6. A crease in George's right back shoulder (no bullet found)

7. A bullet in Dora Thompson's leg

8. A bullet in Nick Zarvos's jawbone

9. A flesh wound on Captain Dothard's stomach (no bullet found)

One bullet was found in the asphalt. How could five bullets cause nine wounds? I have presented the facts so that you may draw your own conclusions.

Later in the day the doctors came up and briefed me on the surgery they had performed. The procedure was explained to me. The spinal cord was opened and the bullet was removed. There were some adhesions, but the spinal cord was not severed at the level of the first lumbar vertebra. They were guardedly optimistic about the long-term outcome.

The area they opened and the area they examined looked good. The nerves were twisted and mangled, but none were cut. However, the bullet had not entered the canal at the L-1 (first lumbar) level. It had entered at the T-12 (twelfth thoracic) level and dropped to the L-1 level.

The doctors looked pleased as they briefed me on the spinal surgery they had performed. I felt encouraged by their optimistic attitude but also disappointed because they could not give me more positive facts about George's paralysis. Their words bounced around in my head: "The area we examined looked good." But they had not opened the spinal canal at T-12, which was the level of entry. X rays revealed no bone fragments at that level and to open it would only risk cutting the other nerves or unnecessarily losing spinal fluid. Also, there is no surgical technique to repair whatever damage had been done there. No one would ever know what damage had been done at the T-12 level.

I finally mustered enough courage to ask, "Will George ever be able to walk again?"

"We believe Governor Wallace will be able to walk with the help of mechanical aids, at the very least with a cane. It is our opinion that he will never walk again in a normal manner."

Unlike polio and multiple sclerosis, which are diseases, or a stroke, which is caused by vascular hemorrhaging of the brain, a spinal-cord injury only paralyzes the body from the point of injury downward. The injury in no way affects the brain. The spinal-cord nerves act as millions of minute communication lines, transmitting messages from the brain to various parts of the body. For example, the brain sends out a signal for the finger to move, and the nerves in the spinal cord transmit the message to the finger, in effect contracting the muscles and tendons to obey the brain's command.

When the nerves in the spinal cord are damaged, the message being sent by the brain is interrupted at the point of injury and does not reach the part of the body for which it is intended. Therefore that part of the body does not respond to the brain's command. You might think of the injury as a washed-out bridge, a blown-up highway or a cut telephone wire.

Mechanically speaking, a damaged spinal cord or cable

should be easily corrected by (a) replacing the damaged wires, (b) splicing the wires together, or (c) bridging over the damaged wires with a jump cable. Scientifically, this has not been achieved, not with real nerves or synthetic ones.

Each case of spinal-cord injury is individual. Each patient has different areas and varying degrees of loss of motor function and sensation. This is why medical reports always seem vague and evasive. In some cases the spinal cord may suffer a contusion, leaving the victim paralyzed only temporarily or partially. Occasionally people have been paralyzed for as long as a year and then experienced a return of motor function. There have been a few isolated cases of paraplegics who have regained their walking ability after several years. But there is no medical explanation for such phenomena. We know one person who regained motor function after three years but still experiences no feeling in his legs. Medical specialists who treat the spinal-cord-injured patient have learned to expect anything. Generally, however, if a person is to regain some motor-function return, the improvement usually occurs within forty-eight hours. If there is no significant change in motor function by twelve to eighteen months, medical experts conclude that the patient is essentially as he will be for the rest of his life. His motor function does not get better or worse—it usually remains unchanged.

Many people expected George to be able to walk after the bullet was removed from his back. They had hoped and prayed for a miracle. We hoped and prayed, too, but for a second miracle. The first one had already happened—George was alive.

Chapter 9

WHEN THE DOCTORS told George that they did not expect him to walk again, he accepted their opinion without emotion. He did not even seem surprised.

He made such a remarkable recovery from his back surgery that he was able to resume his physical therapy program two weeks later. Instead of doing passive exercises in his room, he was taken in a wheelchair to the basement where the physical therapy department was set up. There he was taught the mechanics of the wheelchair: both arms are removable; the footplates swing aside, elevate and can be removed. He learned how to lock the brakes, how to hand-stop the wheels and how to make transfers from the wheelchair to another seat. He began to work at lifting weights to build up his chest and arm muscles. He would have to be able to lift the 150 pounds of his body with his arms.

When George began his weight-lifting exercises he was fitted for braces, and by the time they were made he had developed his torso enough to support his body weight. He was then introduced to the parallel bars. At first it was an agonizing struggle for him to swing down those bars in one direction, but soon he was able to walk the bars both ways in one session. By the time he left Holy Cross Hospital he could go up and down the bars five times.

George's security men, his nurse, Billy Joe and I always accompanied him to his physical therapy classes. Although the parallel exercises were strenuous for George, it was heartening for us to see him on his feet again and we praised him for his accomplishments, loudly applauding each and every time.

Finally George took his first walk outside the parallel bars with only the support of his braces and crutches. To most people it would not have been a pretty sight, but to those of us who loved him and had watched and waited and struggled with him all the way through his illness, it was a glorious event. He had made it!

A few weeks earlier he had tried to joke about how he would roll into the Miami Convention Hall; now he could walk in, if he chose. Politics had never been out of his mind since he was shot, and the Democratic National Convention in Miami was scheduled for July 10. He had been invited by Larry O'Brien to address the convention, an unprecedented move. No presidential candidate had ever been invited to speak at the Democratic Convention before the nominations. This was the same convention that had left the Wallace campaign out of the first draw for hotel rooms.

To improve his appearance for the trip, he began taking sunbaths on the roof of the hospital. This was one of the things I had persuaded him to do after we were married. Sometimes he used to come home despondent because some unthinking person had told him he looked pale, which he interpreted as meaning that his health must be failing. I had convinced him if he had a suntan people would think he was healthy. He tried it and it worked.

George was still having trouble with chronic pain spasms in his side, and he felt so humiliated by being pushed around in a wheelchair that whenever he was pushed to and from his physical therapy he hung his head until his chin touched his chest. As soon as we noticed this awkward habit we called it to his attention so that he could correct it, but he clung to it. Dr. Schanno surmised that the position of the neck bent forward might be giving George relief from the pain in his side.

The convention was not far off, and Dr. Schanno decided his patient needed a trial run. He prescribed a short trip out of the hospital and signed a "pass out" for his patient to have dinner with him at his home. I was staying at a nearby Holiday Inn by this time, and when I learned that George was going to Dr. Schanno's home I was indignant. I felt that I had been generous with my husband, and if he was going to have an evening out it should be with his wife, not his doctor. My time alone with George was long overdue and much needed by both of us. He had been in the hospital two months and we'd been married only eighteen months. I informed George, as was my prerogative, that on his first pass out I expected him to have dinner with me at my motel suite. He could have his second pass out with his doctor.

"But I can't tell my doctor I don't want to go to his house for dinner," George protested.

"You don't have to. Just tell him you'd rather have dinner with your wife in her motel room. He'll understand."

George told Dr. Schanno and he did understand. He even apologized for not thinking of that arrangement himself.

The Alabama security detail, the Secret Service, a nurse and I accompanied George to my suite at the Holiday Inn at Silver Spring. I felt like a schoolgirl on her first date—before the boy is sixteen, with Mother driving, and Daddy and family looking on! The press was aware of our departure and had clocked our time out. It was much like my dorm days at Rollins College. I had a curfew, or rather my escort did. George was like a newborn colt stretching its legs for the first time, a little afraid to stand up. He was anxious and nervous, but I didn't mind. I was so happy I had enough nerve and confidence for both of us. Dinner was prearranged so that George would not have to wait for his meal (I didn't want to waste much time on food, anyhow).

The troupe assisted George with his transfers in and out of the car, then into the motel. They helped him into the living room and positioned his chair comfortably at the table, which was set and ready with fresh flowers. George was concerned about being away from the constant care of his nurses and the relief they could give him from the pain he still suffered, but I shooed the nurse out of the room to a reception room down the hall. I assured her that if George needed anything, I would call her. (Don't call us, we'll call you!) *Toodle-oo!*

We weren't hungry but we ate part of the food on our plates and flushed the rest down the commode so the chef wouldn't be insulted.

As soon as we finished our meal I pushed George's chair

away from the table and swung the footrests back in place. At the hospital George had always allowed the nurses to push him around in the wheelchair. He never offered to do it himself and refused if they insisted. But now he looked at me, smiled, reversed the wheelchair and wheeled into the adjoining bedroom. He didn't seem a bit different from the way he was when he used to walk cockily into a room. It was all in his attitude and the way he did it, not his method of ambulation. I followed George into the bedroom, where he had wheeled up next to the sink and was washing his hands as if he had walked in there. He had not even used the sink in his hospital room but had continued to allow the nurses to wait on him hand and foot, which made me a little angry, because I felt that all that pampering wasn't encouraging him to be independent. I was amazed at the agile way in which George maneuvered about the two rooms. I was also pleased at the transformation in his personality. It wasn't politics that made him push that chair. It was the same thing that motivated Adam.

After he washed and towel-dried his hands, he rolled his chair over to one of the beds and parked alongside it. He had clearly become the aggressor now, which made me feel uncertain and very feminine in his company. He locked the brakes on his wheelchair and removed both side arms. Then he looked at me and threw open both arms in a wide, inviting gesture. I ran to him and fell across his lap and into his arms. We kissed with a passion, a longing and a hunger equal to that of the reunited POW husbands and their wives. We hugged and kissed and cried and sobbed.

After we collected ourselves a bit, I called in the security men to put George in bed so that he could be more comfortable while he watched television. As they left the room I locked the door, bolted the latch, turned off the television set and returned to the arms of my waiting husband.

George was back in the hospital on time and in much better spirits than when he left. His wheelchair had a new wiggle in its roll—and I had a new bounce in my walk.

The next afternoon we attended a picnic at Dr. Schanno's house. We weren't trying to hide from the press but frankly there was no way to handle that many people at Dr. Schanno's house and the Secret Service did not want our destination disclosed. We had a delightful time with the Schannos and their eight children, but toward the end of our visit the hospital called to inform us that the press had learned the location of the Schanno home and were headed in our direction. George, not expecting to be photographed, had worn his pajamas and bathrobe, so Mary Jane, Dr. Schanno's wife, made a rapid tour through her husband's wardrobe and emerged with a pair of brown trousers, a gold knit shirt and a silk ascot. (During the first few weeks, George had lost so much weight that in his pictures he looked especially haggard around the neck, so we always tucked an ascot into his shirt when he was being photographed.) Dr. Schanno's clothes fit to a T and we didn't try to hide the house slippers. Sure enough, when we said good-bye at the front door, the television cameras were ready and rolling.

George was at Holy Cross Hospital for fifty-four days. During our last few days there we all were excited and busy making preparations for our trip to Miami. I did my usual last-minute, one-stop shopping for myself and the children. The remainder of my personal time I saved for the big beauty treatment at the local salon. Shopping for George was not as easy. I was forced to call in a tailor to get his wardrobe in shape because none of his old clothes fit. The muscles in his upper torso and neck had become so enlarged from exercising that the collars of his shirts would not meet at the neck. The hip band on the leg braces, together with the stomach bandages, required four more inches in the waist of his trousers. He was brace-walking every day and had been putting the braces on over his casual slacks, which was fine for the practice sessions. But we envisioned him either walking into Convention Hall with his braces on or at least standing at the podium to make his speech, and the braces simply had to go under his trousers. By the time the tailor had made several trips to the hospital to take correct measurements, he realized he had not been hired to do a tailoring job but to perform an engineering feat. Each shoe is permanently attached to the metal braces, and it is almost impossible to pull a pair of trousers over them. The tailor's ingenuity ran out. Nothing he thought up would work. Finally someone in the physiotherapy department remembered a tailor who had custom-designed suits for a paraplegic.

Together the two tailors solved the problem: They inserted zippers in the inside seam of the trousers.

Although we were glad to be leaving, we hated to say good-bye to the loving, caring, wonderful friends we had made at Holy Cross. They were the people who had seen a stranger brought in on a stretcher and had watched his slow, laborious recovery with a prayer in their hearts and a word of cheer on their lips. Each of them had, in some way, played a part in George's miraculous recovery.

Two nights before our departure Sister Helen Marie organized a proper farewell. We were to have a special Mass in the hospital chapel, followed by a dinner in the banquet room. The meal was planned with great care. Decorative cloths and fruits adorned the tables, place cards and wine glasses were set at each plate and special cake was baked. The Mass was to be performed in English, interspersed with hymns familiar to all.

On the evening of the ceremonies, just before we went downstairs to the chapel, Sister Helen Marie and Sister Maurita Hartney, C.S.C., a visiting sister, came to George's room. George had come to know and love both these nuns, who had made frequent brief visits to his room, forever cheerful and always with a word of encouragement. They had reinforced his faith and prayed at his bedside, but, most important, they had given him hope. Now they presented him with a printed copy of the Mass. About halfway down the page we saw George's name and beside it the words: Twenty-third Psalm. George was reluctant to participate in the service but the good sisters assured him he would do just fine.

After they left the room George confided to me that he had serious doubts about whether he would be able to find the voice to speak the lines. I told him not to worry, to start the psalm, and if he got to a place where he couldn't continue I would finish it for him. I sincerely hoped I wouldn't have to do that, but I thought it might give him confidence to know that he had an understudy ready and waiting in the wings.

Billy Joe beckoned for us to start downstairs. Governor and Mrs. Mandel were waiting for us in the corridor to the chapel; so was the television crew who would film the Mass. As we approached the door to the chapel, George gave me a very uncertain look and tugged on me to lean down.

"I don't think I'm going to be able to do this," he whispered.

"You'll do fine," I said.

I kissed him on the cheek and squeezed his hand. Sister Maurita was playing the organ as we made our way to the front row and found our seats. Halfway through the program George was already brushing away the tears as they rolled down his cheeks, and I didn't see how either of us would make it through the Mass because the understudy had a wet face, too.

When it was time for George to participate in the program, the security men rolled his chair to the front of the altar, then returned to their places. The tears in my eyes blurred the sad picture of his frail, pitifully wounded body.

George adjusted his black-rimmed bifocals and began to read:

"The Lord is my shepherd; I shall not want. He maketh me to lie down in green pastures: he leadeth me beside the still waters. He restoreth my soul. . . ."

His voice was weak and shaky as he halted at each phrase.

"He leadeth me in the paths of righteousness for his name's sake. Yea, though I walk through the valley of the shadow of death—"

George's voice broke off, he was so overcome with emotion. God, please let him finish, because I can't! I prayed. I had stopped trying to fight the tears.

"I will fear no evil"—His voice choked again—"for thou art with me; thy rod and thy staff they comfort me. Thou preparest a table before me In the presence of mine enemies"—a chill went up my spine; yes, he had plenty of political enemies—"thou anointest my head with oil; my cup runneth over."

George stopped to wipe his eyes with a wadded-up white handkerchief, then continued.

"Surely goodness and mercy shall follow me all the days of my life"—surely you deserve goodness, for you have made a supreme sacrifice, I thought—"And I will dwell in the house of the Lord for ever. Amen."

On the day we left, the Holy Cross staff gathered at the front door. They all were there to say farewell—the lab technician, the janitor, the respiratory therapist, the cooks, the nurses, the aides, the LPNs and the RNs, the doctors, the sisters, the chaplain, the office workers and the members of the hospital board—just as they all had been there to perform the services that helped him get well and enabled him to live. They waved and cried and cheered as Sister Helen Marie escorted us to the waiting limousine. When George was settled comfortably inside the car, she took his hand in both of hers. "Goodbye, Governor Wallace, God bless you," she said. Then she kissed him.

As we drove away, George and I waved and smiled through our tears. The tears would dry and disappear, but the memory of Holy Cross would stay with us forever.

Chapter 10

At ANDREWS AIR FORCE BASE, a huge medical evacuation airplane was waiting for us. President Nixon had been kind enough to make the use of governmental medical facilities available to George immediately after he was shot, and since we considered the President's generosity more protocol than political, we did not hesitate to accept any offer we felt we needed. We accepted the use of the medivac plane because it would make the trip more comfortable for George.

As soon as we boarded the plane, George was placed on a little stretcher in the forward section of the cabin, where two Air Force nurses attended him. Our destination was Miami—but first we would make one stop in Alabama so that George could attend the Democratic National Convention with his governorship fully restored.

In a way I dreaded the stop in Montgomery because I knew it would be an emotional scene. All our friends and many of our relatives would be there, and I knew that when they saw George their grief over his accident would materialize into tears. The people who loved George would not be able to contain their anguish when they looked upon their once mighty head of state reduced to an invalid in a wheelchair. We had heard that people were coming by the busloads to the Dannelly Field Airport. Others had driven from all parts of the state to be there when their Governor arrived home at last.

I worried most for George's mother, "Miss Mozelle." I was

also afraid that when she embraced her wounded son he would be so overcome with emotion that he would not be able to go through the ceremony of accepting the power of the governorship. All that was required of George to resume his role as governor was to touch the Alabama soil, but his loyal followers wanted a glimpse of their too-long-absent leader and an opportunity to express their love, support and sympathy. I pleaded with our staff for no ceremony at all, but the people would not be denied the voice of their chosen one. I extracted two firm promises from the staff: No one would physically approach George during his stop, and the reunion with his mother would be delayed until after his speech.

George was miserable during the entire trip. The nurses did everything to make him comfortable but his anxiety mounted. His pain would not come under control. Our plane was crowded with staff and press and I tried unsuccessfully to keep his cabin curtains closed. One reporter's version of George's reactions on the airplane was published, unabridged. It was a complete, detailed description of every move he made, even down to the method and frequency of urination.

About two weeks before George was released from the hospital he had begun to have crying spells. He was also depressed. As these spells persisted, his physicians prescribed medication to elevate his moods. There was, however, no pill to cure or even alter the growing realization that he would remain paralyzed, perhaps for the rest of his life.

Thirty minutes before we landed, I went to George's cabin and stood beside his stretcher. I held his hands tightly, trying to impart to him whatever strength and courage I could muster. He cried unashamedly.

"I can't face all my friends. I'm not up to it," he said.

"You'll have to try."

"I'm afraid I won't be able to talk."

"Don't worry about it. You really don't have to say anything, anyhow. And if you can't talk, I'll do it for you."

"No, I'll do it myself," he said, with a new resolve.

As the plane began making its descent I returned to my seat and fastened the seat belt across my lap. Through my window I could see the Montgomery airport. The buses were parked in a row and cars lined both sides of the Selma Highway leading to the airport as far as I could see. A mass of people waited near the private terminal. Later we learned that some of them had been there since early morning.

While we were saying our last good-byes at Holy Cross, stringent security preparations were already underway in Montgomery. The Secret Service, sensitive to the possibility of a second attempt on George's life, had decided to strengthen the protective measures for his first public appearance. The crowd was to be kept a good distance away from him, newsmen and newswomen were to be bodily searched before entering the press area, and only persons wearing a special security lapel pin would be allowed inside the ropes which held back the crowds. These restrictions even kept George's Aunt Merle and my seventy-year-old Aunt Thelma behind the ropes, sweltering in the 90-degree temperature, along with hundreds of state employees. George's return had caused an exodus at the state building exceeded only by a state holiday, and the Capitol was virtually deserted. The always-open door to the governor's office was locked and a sign posted outside read, "Gone to the airport."

I could see the outline of a small platform almost marking the spot where George and I had waited in the back seat of the car that morning of May 15. He had been so healthy, so vital, so cocky and self-sure. The way he had stared out the window, puffing on his cigar, created an aura of strength. Even his arrogance had a certain appeal. It hardly seemed possible that this man I was coming home with was the same man with whom I had departed only weeks before. Dear God, it didn't seem real! It seemed as if we were returning from a two-month-long bad dream.

The thud of the tires screeching on the runway shook me from my trance. It was no dream. All this had really happened. I gripped the chair arms, bracing my head against the headrest as the reverse thrust slowed the momentum of the aircraft. The plane taxied off the main runway and onto a smaller lane. It came to a full stop at 11 A.M., our estimated time of arrival.

When I returned to George's cabin, all the confidence he had regained had been swept away by another wave of emotion. "Brace up, darling," I whispered.

115

George was lifted from his stretcher and placed in his wheelchair. A nurse helped him adjust his tie and combed his hair. The ramp was rolled out of the side of the aircraft for George to deplane. I could hear Dr. Robert Strong of Trinity Presbyterian Church, the minister who married us, giving the invocation. A heavy canvas curtain hid George from the view of the crowd and at the same time hid the tears running down his face. As the Troy State University band came to the last bars of the national anthem, the curtain was pulled aside and Captain Dothard gently eased the wheelchair down the ramp. Four Phantom jets from the Alabama Air National Guard flew over in a formation salute to their commander in chief. Lieutenant Governor Jere Beasley reached out and shook George's hand as he touched the ground. In George's other hand was the rumpled white handkerchief.

The 3,500 people who had gathered let out a loud, sustained cheer as George made his way to the speaker's platform and up the ramp. This was the first time I had seen a political gathering where everyone was crying, including the speaker. George looked as though he would remain that way.

"George, do you want me to speak for you?" I asked.

Without acknowledging my question he began.

"Ladies and gentlemen, fellow Alabamians, it's great to be back in the state again. . . ."

His voice was weak and his delivery was a bit slow and deliberate. He thanked everyone for the many kindnesses they had shown him during his illness. Then, when he complimented the Holy Cross staff for the fine treatment they had given him, his voice broke off for a moment and he completely stopped talking. I stood still, waiting for the sound of his voice. I didn't know how he would be able to continue. All he had to add was, "It's good to be home, folks," and let it go at that.

The network television cameras, which were carrying his return to Alabama on a live telecast, continued to roll. What a disaster if George broke down in front of millions of viewers. I agonized every silent second, remembering how strong and vital he had been on the day we left this same airport to go to Maryland.

Then George wiped his eyes, took a deep breath and

plunged into a full-scale political speech. His voice was not strong, but it was firm, and when he commented on the little man being taxed to death, he punctuated the phrase with almost the same force that was his trademark. George spoke for a full twenty minutes. He was truly a professional and it showed.

I looked forward to Miami. It would be the best medicine we could give him.

On the way to the Democratic National Convention in Miami, I asked George if he was sure he felt up to making his appearance before the delegates. He replied, "I promised the people that I would carry their message, and that's what I intend to do when I speak before the convention. If the party doesn't change its direction, it will lose in November, and I intend to tell them this one last time." His mind was made up.

All during George's hospital stay in Maryland the one goal that had kept him moving ahead was the convention in Miami. Now the goal was at hand.

The Wallace Campaign Headquarters was in the Sheraton Four Ambassadors and the hotel management went to great lengths to make our accommodations as comfortable as possible. Governor Reuben Askew and the University of Miami had furnished our suite with a hospital bed and physical therapy equipment so that George would not have to interrupt his exercise routine. When we arrived at the suite we were greeted by our friend Bill France, president of the National Association of Stock Car Auto Racing and head of the Florida delegation. He had prepared a very special surprise: Marty Robbins was serenading us with his ballad "El Paso" as we entered the room. It was a refreshing change from the dreary, tiresome hospital days to which we had become all too accustomed.

Miami gave us an opportunity for a family reunion. Mother, my brother Charles and his wife, Betty Joyce, were there and so were all the Wallaces. The strength of the Wallace family is amazing. They helped immeasurably in Miami, as they had in all of George's previous campaigns.

The second night after our arrival we went downstairs to host a reception for our campaign workers, friends and delegates. Ferlin Husky, our personal friend, the country singer who scored two hits with "Gone" and "Wings of a Dove," furnished the music and remained with us for the rest of the week. Lee made her first televised speech. It was thirty seconds long and she wrote it herself. George attended two press conferences, took an afternoon boat cruise and met with delegates each day. The rest of the time he remained in his room, seeing only his family, a few friends and the Alabama press corps. I regretted all my invitations and interviews because I felt George needed all of my attention and support.

On the eve of his appearance at the convention, I was astonished that en route to the auditorium George extended his arms from the open window of the moving limousine to shake hands with strangers, many of whom wore hippie-type clothes. He obviously experienced no fear of crowds as a result of the shooting. The Secret Service agents, the Alabama security men and I, still suffering anxiety, insisted that he keep his hands in the car.

Upon arriving at the auditorium, Lee turned to her father and said, "Daddy, are you going to speak at a political rally?"

George replied, "No, darling, I have been to one political rally too many."

George had to wait backstage for almost an hour before the chairman introduced him. The hot, stuffy air made him perspire profusely and the nagging pain in his side bent him over in his wheelchair. The longer we waited, the more his tension increased, and once again it appeared that he would not be able to make his speech. But this time there was no one who could bail him out. Certainly not I. At one point he became nauseated and almost fainted. Dr. George Traugh, a doctor of physical rehabilitation medicine from the University of Alabama Rehabilitation Center, had accompanied us to the convention hall. He took measures to revive his patient; a glass of orange juice gave George a spurt of energy.

I took my seat in the governor's box along with Lee and George's mother a few minutes before George was presented to the delegates. When his chair was wheeled into position at the podium the forward thrust almost pushed him over the speaker's stand. I was nervous and proud, forcing a smile and fighting tears. Once again George warned the Democratic Party to change their liberal ways and listen to the voice of the people. If the audience had known the immense personal struggle of the man before them, they would have had an even keener appreciation of the dramatic presentation he made.

This was not a happy time for George, particularly after the convention did not accept any of the planks of his message. It was then that he said, "They can't win." He had foreseen the disaster that resulted in November.

For the rest of the trip I stayed in the suite with him, refusing even the request from Bob Strauss, who is now the chairman of the Democratic Party, to appear on the Democratic Telethon and begging off with a promise to appear the next time, which I did in 1974. Four doctors had been keeping a close check on George's physical condition throughout the convention and his three private nurses were on constant call. When the doctors discovered a new oozing of pus from the old midsection scar, they insisted that we remove George to the University of Alabama Hospital in Birmingham as soon as possible. They suspected a new abscess.

George and I had had only a few private moments together in our hotel suite. When we learned that he would be reentering the hospital for another long stay, we both became very distressed over the need to be separated again. George had never wanted to go to the university rehabilitation center at all. He was homesick and weary of hospitals, but mostly he and I just wanted to be together. At the onset of his crying spells at Holy Cross, his doctors had recommended that he bypass a standard rehabilitation hospital and return home instead, where he could enlist the aid of a private physical therapist and set up a routine at home. Psychologically that would have been the best treatment, but medically it was impossible because of the new abscess.

George and I called Dr. Traugh into our room for a private discussion. We explained to him the anxieties we both were suffering from the prolonged separation and openly professed to him our acute need to be together. We begged him to make arrangements for me to stay in a room at the hospital, but the rehab center was overcrowded and no rooms were available.

In accordance with Dr. Traugh's urging, we left Miami one

day earlier than we had originally planned. On the day of our departure George called his top campaign people to his bedside and commended them all for the way they had carried on in spite of the fact that their candidate had been incapacitated. Not easily deterred, they cheerfully spoke of a new effort for 1976.

When we left Miami our spirits were a little down. Senator George McGovern had won the Democratic nomination, Senator Tom Eagleton had been selected Vice-Presidential nominee, and the party had rejected the minority planks George had proposed. George doubted the Democratic Party would be successful in November. Our letdown was not from losing the political battle but from losing the goal that we had been using to motivate George. There was no longer the convention to look forward to.

PART II

Chapter 11

SOME PEOPLE have marveled at the way I adapted to the role of governor's wife. Others have sneered at my overeager political inclinations. Few of them realize that I was born on the fringes of politics and that fate twice thrust me into the center of its arena. Tragic circumstances were involved both times. In more recent years it was the death of Lurleen Wallace and my subsequent marriage to the widowed George Wallace. In earlier years it was the death of Sarah Carnley Folsom, wife of my Uncle James Folsom, which necessitated that my family live with him.

Sarah Carnley Folsom died from complications of childbirth in 1944, leaving Uncle Jim with the care of two little daughters, four-year-old Rachel and sixteen-month-old Melissa. He was living in Cullman, a small town in north Alabama. The Folsom home was in Elba, a small town in south Alabama, but my uncle had moved to Cullman to help establish an insurance company that was organized and owned by the Folsom family.

For a while after Aunt Sarah's death, members of both the Carnley and Folsom families helped to look after the two little girls, but since all the relatives lived 250 miles south of Cullman, the distance caused a hardship for them. The girls would stay in Elba for a while until one of the relatives was able to take them back to Cullman and care for them there. Finally my uncle declared that he intended to have his daughters live with him in Cullman and that was that. Whoever looked after the girls would have to do it in north Alabama.

My grandmother, Eulala Cornelia Dunnavant Folsom, had been widowed for twenty-five years and, although she was sixty-nine years old, she agreed to move up to Cullman and keep house for her youngest son. Granny made a valiant effort, but the task was too much for her. She had a slight stroke and was forced to return to Elba.

James Elisha Folsom and Ruby Lee Folsom were the last of Eulala's seven living children. All of her children had blue eyes and black hair—although some were blond as infants—and were tall. Ruby was the youngest and the shortest child, being five feet ten and a half inches barefooted. James, next youngest, who became known affectionately as "Big Jim," outstripped the others in size and height and stood a full six feet six inches tall.

Ruby and James were as close as twins and looked enough alike to have been twins. Ruby worshiped her brother. He had been kind to her and tried to help her overcome the tremendous inferiority complex she had because of her height. Ruby and James were six and eight years old when their father died, and they developed a close bond in their childhood that carried over into their adult years.

Granny was not physically able to go back to Cullman after her stroke. Someone had to help James with his children. His other sister, Thelma, had no children but she had to remain in Elba to nurse Granny back to health. That left my mother, Ruby.

My father, Charles Ellis, was a civil engineer and at the time was working on a highway project. Since his job demanded that we move frequently, it was not difficult for Daddy to arrange to be transferred near Cullman.

The Ellis family home place was in Bullock County, several miles west of Union Springs at Shopton Community. My grandfather, George Ellis, and my grandmother, Lena Arant Ellis, owned a dairy farm; forty Negro hands milked the cows in exchange for a humble dwelling and whatever food they could grow. Papa George and Mama Lena had eight children—Grady, Bessie, Ruby, Ethel, Eula, Charlie, Walter and Virginia, in that order. They were Methodists and were mild-mannered people compared to the forceful personalities of the Folsoms. All the children left the farm except Walter, who stayed to manage the dairy. Daddy had been working as an assistant civil engineer on a highway project between Elba and Opp when he met and married my mother.

When all the arrangements were made, Mother, Daddy, my brother, Charles, and I moved to Cullman. We lived with my Uncle Jimmy and my cousins, Rachel and Melissa, in a big, two-story, white frame house catty-cornered across the street from the elementary school.

Living with Uncle Jimmy was like having the story of Paul Bunyan come to life. And like the legendary logman, Uncle Jimmy's supersized frame made him a folk hero in his own time. His mere presence commanded the attention and respect of all those around him, and although I saw him all the time I never ceased to be awed by his giant figure.

He loved children and knew how to enjoy them. Somehow he managed to distribute his affection and attention equally among Rachel, Melissa, Charles and me. He was in the habit of taking long walks for exercise, usually with the four of us skipping along, trying to keep up with his long-legged gait. One of his favorite ways to entertain us was to demonstrate his mysterious ear-wiggling technique, which we considered pure magic because none of us could imitate it. We had the most fun playing a game called "Skin the Rabbit." Each of us would bend over in front of him with our head and hands between our legs and he would jerk us up by the hands, flip us over in the air and lower us into an upright position with our feet on the ground. From the sidelines it must have looked as if our heads would crack the floor, but Uncle Jimmy lifted us safely every time. The brush with danger was part of the thrill, and we squealed and pleaded for him to "Do it again! Do it again!"

Cullman was a German settlement nestled in the foothills of the Appalachian Mountains. In contrast to the large black-labored plantations in central and south Alabama, the hardworking German landowners farmed their own small rocky acreage. Consequently there was no black population at all in Cullman County. The industrious German women did their own housework.

Mother ran the thirteen-room house with the strength of

125

an Amazon, but without the loss of her femininity. She had never been without a mammy for her children and soon hired a young German girl to assist her with the heavy cleaning. Mother told all of us children that we would have to help with the household chores and assigned each of us a small job. Since I was the oldest girl, by six months, I was given the responsibility of taking care of Rachel and Melissa, which made me feel grown up.

One day soon after we moved to Cullman, Mother called Charles and me aside for a private conference. I thought she was singling us out for a special privilege, since we were her natural-born children, but what she had to say to us was deeper and more profound than I had imagined. She started by saying that she loved us very much and because she was our real mother we should know that already. Then she said, "Rachel and Melissa don't have a mother. I hope I don't have to make any difference in you children, but if I ever do, I'll have to make it in favor of Rachel and Melissa." Having been assured of her love, we accepted her proposal. Under the circumstances it seemed reasonable enough.

Like most little girls, I loved my daddy very much. He called me "Miss Babes," a term of endearment he used so often I cannot remember hearing him call me by my name. Daddy had black hair, brown eyes and an olive complexion. He was an expert fly-fisherman, and in the summers he fished so much that the freckles on his arms ran together, making his skin even darker. He was five feet eight inches tall, and while his shortness was undoubtedly a problem for him—having married into a family of oversized people—it was my salvation. Otherwise I might have been a giant.

Daddy was away much of the time but when he was home he turned his engineering skills to making kites for all of us. He used limbs from trees and brown-paper grocery bags to make his winged wonders, and we gathered up the materials for him, ransacking the house for scraps of cloth to use for tails. On a good windy day Daddy would make us a sophisticated box kite. I was impressed with his ability to take nothing and make something out of it, and I think this may have been the basis for my early curiosity about things mechanical.

126

A girl for Mother and a boy for Daddy: Charles and me in 1948.

Rachel, Melissa and I pose in our first inaugural clothes (left).
Playing the gypsy for Halloween at age four (right).

No matter how hard he tried, Daddy could not outmeasure the Folsoms. Neither could any of his achievements match those of Jim Folsom, who was the yardstick by which my mother measured all men.

While Daddy tolerated the living situation in Cullman, my mother thrived on the challenge. She ran the house, cooked the meals and managed the children, and whenever she could she threw parties. She had always made pretty dresses for me, but after we moved to Cullman she didn't have as much time to sew. One summer she decided to make Rachel, Melissa and me some new velvet dresses for the winter, and when she tried mine on me to see if it fit, I thought the dress was so pretty I wanted to wear it right away.

Mother tried to reason with me. "C'nelia, you can't wear this dress now, it's too hot."

Determined to wear the dress in spite of the sweltering weather, I answered, "This dress won't be too hot, Mother—I'll put it in the refrigerator."

All the Folsoms love music, and traditionally most of them have played at least one instrument. Grandpa Folsom played the fiddle, but neither Jim nor Ruby mastered anything musical except the radio and phonograph, although they played the daylights out of their store-bought music boxes. I could sing every word of "Shoofly Pie and Apple Pan Dowdy," although I didn't understand it then and I don't now. We all used to pull the stops and pump away on the old church organ Mother had picked up on one of her antique outings. Finally I began to spend a lot of time pounding the keys of the piano my Aunt Sarah had left as part of her estate and which my Uncle Jimmy kept in the living room in hopes that his daughters might be as musically inclined as their mother had been.

Mother was delighted to learn that she had a young virtuoso in the family. Bent on developing my talent, she convinced Mrs. Douglas Lovelace to take me on as a piano student although I was only six years old and Mrs. Lovelace preferred not to take children until they were eight. I worked especially hard to prove that she had not made a mistake by lifting her rule.

A year before I was born, Uncle Jimmy had made his first

bid for the United States Congress, and Mother campaigned for him the entire nine months she carried me. Two years later he made his second bid for the congressional seat. He lost both times. As a result of Daddy's work, we lived in almost every little town in south Alabama, and wherever we lived everybody soon knew Ruby Folsom Ellis and heard about her politically ambitious brother.

After his two unsuccessful bids for Congress, Uncle Jim launched his first campaign for the Alabama governorship in 1942. He ran second, which surprised everyone (except my mother) since he was relatively unknown on the statewide level. According to my mother, Uncle Jimmy would have won that race if he had taken his brother's advice and used poll watchers on Election Day.

By the time we moved to Cullman, Uncle Jimmy was oiling his campaign machinery for the 1946 governor's race. Actually he had never let it collect any rust. His move to Cullman, aside from the insurance business, was a way for him to capture the north Alabama vote, where the voter population was much heavier. What better way to meet the voters than by selling insurance door to door?

Uncle Jimmy ran his campaign out of his house or out of his car, whichever place he happened to be at the time. When her brother was on the road, Mother kept the campaign going at home. She juggled her dual roles with the agility of a trapeze artist. She ran the house with a frying pan in one hand and a telephone in the other.

The dining-room table was always full of campaign literature, boxes of envelopes and letters to the voters from the candidate. My uncle's favorite mailing list was that of the rural-route box holders. It was important to secure the heavy rural vote and one way to do that was to send the country folks a letter. We didn't eat a meal on that table for months. That wasn't so bad, but when the backlog of literature threatened to take over the breakfast table, we worked twice as hard to get the material off the table and into the hands of the voters. We folded letters, stuffed them in the envelopes, licked the envelopes and licked the stamps. We did everything by hand as there were no folding machines in those days.

Sometimes we went with Uncle Jimmy into the rural areas to the speakings, as a political rally was called in those days. Most of them were held in country school buildings. The people who came to hear the gubernatorial candidates were farmers and they usually wore their overalls and work boots. I helped pass out pamphlets listing what Uncle Jimmy was for and what he was against. Then, later on in his speech when he would make a pitch for contributions, I would grab a wooden suds bucket and go into the crowd and pass the bucket. Uncle Jimmy would hold up one of his suds buckets and a corn-shuck mop and promise that if he were elected he would clean all the dirt and corruption out of the Capitol. When we returned home from the rallies our help was again solicited to count the pennies, nickels and dimes that had been dropped in the suds buckets. That's how Jim Folsom financed all his campaigns. His idea was to let the little men invest in government.

When we weren't helping with the campaign, Rachel, Melissa, Charles and I spent all our time playing across the street on the school grounds where the playground equipment was more fun than the toys we had at home. I loved riding the spinning jenny. I would lie down on the bench with my face toward the sky, dangling my feet and giving the thing a push. Then I'd study the images in the swirling clouds and try to give each one a name. Those beautiful billowing clouds gave me deep appreciation of God and the beautiful wondrous universe he created for us to enjoy. I searched those blue skies and wondered how far beyond those clouds one would have to go to find God. He never seemed too far away.

One day when all four of us children were skating on the school sidewalk, I got into my first political fight. Two senior high school girls were also skating on the sidewalk and they asked us our names. When Rachel told them her last name was Folsom, the bigger girl said she couldn't stand that mean Big Jim Folsom who was running for governor. Rachel started to cry and the girls skated off, laughing. As they turned their backs to us I stuck my tongue out at the bigger girl only to have her turn around and catch me in the act. She skated back and grabbed my arm, twisting it behind my back. Being a first-grader I was no physical match for her, so I screamed, but the louder

I screamed the harder she twisted my arm. I refused to take back the insult and she refused to let me go until Mother came and warned her she'd better pick on someone her own size. When Uncle Jimmy won the governor's race, my greatest satisfaction was imagining that girl's disappointment.

Uncle Jimmy campaigned on a populist platform, promising to pave the dirt roads from the farms to the towns so that the farmers could get their produce to market. He also promised to raise old-age pension checks, increase schoolteacher salaries and remove the restrictive poll tax so that people could vote without having to pay for the privilege.

It was the custom for gubernatorial candidates to stop and make speeches at every county seat and crossroad as they made their swing through the state. That type of campaigning was called "stumping," because sometimes the only stage a politician could find was a tree stump. In those days, when there was no such thing as television, one had to stump to be elected to state office in Alabama.

The preferred places to make a speech were a schoolhouse, a courthouse or a street corner. Uncle Jimmy did them all, but he added a new twist to the traditional type of campaign. He would stop at a farmhouse, sit down at the table and have a meal while he told the folks what he planned to do for the rural areas. In a matter of days everybody in the county would be talking about how Big Jim stopped at the Sawyers' place. One day he drank a glass of buttermilk with a family while he listened to their problems. He promised that if they would help him get elected governor he would pave the dirt road in front of their house. After he won he fulfilled his promise of paving the road and he appropriately named it Buttermilk Road.

Mother did as much politicking as she did cooking and it was a good thing she did because she spared her brother the misfortune of being dropped from the official list of runoff candidates in the 1946 governor's race. Uncle Jimmy had sent his campaign expense papers to Sybil Poole, the Alabama Secretary of State, several days before the specified deadline for candidates to formally file these statements. Early in the day before the midnight deadline Sybil Poole noticed that she had not received Jim Folsom's papers. Knowing that Jim was in fact the leading candidate she decided to call the Folsom home in Cullman to check. Ruby answered the phone.

"But Jim sent his papers several days ago," she said. "I don't understand. Are you sure you didn't receive them?"

"There's no mistake. If Jim is going to be qualified before midnight I suggest you send another statement and have it hand-delivered to me. I'll wait at the office for it."

Mother did as she was advised and Jim was qualified. That particular act of quick-wittedness gave Mother reason to claim for years how she held the ladder while Jim Folsom hung the moon.

Upon his election in November 1946, Uncle Jimmy not only became the youngest governor to date in the history of Alabama but also acquired the distinction of being the youngest governor in the United States. There was much speculation about the possibility of his marriage and a new first lady for the state. To squelch the rumors Jim Folsom announced soon after his election that his sister Ruby would serve as his official hostess. To avoid having his name romantically linked with anyone in particular he decided to escort his sister to the inaugural ball, and together they led the grand march.

After the first dance, which was reserved for the new governor and his lady, Uncle Jimmy made the rounds and danced with most of the other women, lifting them off their feet as he whirled them around the floor. We children were allowed to attend the ball, and Daddy did the box step with me, Rachel and Melissa, exactly as we had rehearsed. Charles wouldn't dance. He thought we were silly.

Inauguration Day was cold, but that didn't cool the spirits of the thousands of people who lined the streets for the four-hour parade. Rachel, Melissa and I wore dresses of identical design in soft green, blue and pink wool. We sported new, brown, genuine-alligator baby-doll shoes and Buster Brown hats. Numb from the cold, we kept our coats on and wrapped our legs in blankets. Knowing that everyone would be watching us, we exhibited model behavior, except for the times when Uncle Jimmy's inaugural address got too deep for us and we read funny books. We had been coached so well that when a newspaper man asked me if I was having a good time, I looked at him wide-eyed and said, "No comment."

Life in the Governor's Mansion was like a circus with a featured act going on in all three rings at the same time. There was glitter, glamour, thrills and excitement. Uncle Jim espoused an Andrew Jackson philosophy of opening the Mansion to the public. In keeping with his philosophy, Mother threw lavish parties and teas and saw to it that her guest list always included people who had never before been to the Governor's Mansion.

The house was tastefully appointed with fine antiques, Persian rugs, Venetian glass chandeliers, gold-leaf mirrors, Bavarian crystal, Spode china, Spanish lace tablecloths and a Federalist sterling silver tea service. The floors were waxed and shined until they reflected images. (They also caught visitors unaware and occasionally one would wind up sprawled in the middle of the sparkling hardwood.) There was a massive grand staircase that branched off in opposite directions at the first landing. We children kept its mahogany banisters polished by applying the seat of our pants every day on the way down to breakfast.

Mother might have lacked for household help in Cullman, but she was overrun with servants in Montgomery. We had one chauffeur, one cook, two maids and two butlers. Our table was always served formally, even for breakfast. When a guest came to call at the Mansion a butler answered the door wearing white gloves and carrying a small flat silver tray in one hand. In those days everyone carried small white cards on which his full name was engraved. When the butler politely asked, "May I say who is calling, please?" he extended the silver tray to receive the card. The guest was then directed to a sitting room and invited to be seated, after which the butler would say, "I will announce you." This was not an unusual custom in the finer homes of Montgomery during those days. The capital city was still a very Southern town, untouched by outsiders moving in and inhabited by old families with an air of stilted aristocracy. Even at the age of eight, when I was dressed to go visiting, I carried my own calling cards. There was no such thing as a shopping center in Montgomery, and ladies never went to town without their hats and gloves.

There were no security guards at the Mansion, no fences or gates to keep people out, and no fancy alarm or surveillance systems. Although people lined the halls and flooded the reception room to see the Governor every day at his office, no one ever took the liberty of invading the privacy of his home without a proper invitation. People had restraint in those days, and they exercised it.

Christmas was a festive season. Our tree was a twelve-foot-high Alabama cedar. It was not as pretty or symmetrical as a spruce or short-leaf pine, but it was homegrown, and to use any other kind was an unforgivable sin in Mother's eyes. Mother did the decorating herself and no room was spared her talented touch. Plastic greenery was unheard of and in good garden-club tradition she used fresh pine boughs, smilax, holly and mistletoe. She created a beautiful forest scene in Charles's room by using Spanish moss sprinkled with homemade (Ivory Snow) snow. Mother let her talent overcome her common sense in that display and the beauty of the scene was almost overshadowed by the consequences my brother suffered. Mother didn't realize that she had forgotten to shake the Spanish moss until my brother was covered with chigger bites and had to evacuate his room to escape the ants, spiders and bugs. Well, you can't say Mother didn't create a realistic forest scene for a little boy who loved the woods and hunting.

There was a touch of politics in every part of our lives and Christmas was no exception. Before the guests arrived for the Christmas parties, Mother took a tube of her brightest red lipstick and, stealing a theme from Uncle Jim's campaign speeches, wrote in large letters on every mirror in the Mansion, "Merry Christmas to you and you and you."

In the midst of her Christmas decorating and entertaining Mother seized an opportunity to give her children a lesson in human kindness. She accepted an invitation for us to attend a special performance of Christmas songs and the reenactment of the birth of Christ with scripture readings. What we saw was an earnest, sincere rendition of the familiar Christmas story. But this Christmas program was different from any others we had seen. It was performed by convicted criminals inside the women's state prison. We were touched by their humbleness.

Although some of the women were crying they seemed

gladdened by the fact that the Governor's family had taken the time to share Christmas with them. It was obvious that our presence had caused them to put a little something extra into their presentation. I learned that criminals are vulnerable to human emotions, too. They yearn, cry, want, need, love, hurt, suffer the same as other people.

In many states the executive mansions are staffed and supplied by the state prison system, especially when the prison is located near the capital city, as happened to be the case in Alabama. Most of our servants at the Mansion were trusties from the state penitentiary assigned there as a reward for good behavior. Usually the ones who worked for us had been convicted of murder in crimes of passion—usually a triangle situation involving a wife, a husband and a lover. The person who commits this type of crime usually does not commit murder again, as he has vented his hostility upon the person who offended him rather than on society. This type of inmate was preferred because the problem of theft was eliminated.

Rachel and Melissa and I each had a nurse. All were trusties from Tutwiler Prison. The one who looked after me was called Anna. Each night the nurses would put all three of us in a tub full of bubble bath and let us play for a while; then they would rub us dry with a big, soft towel and help us get into our nightgowns. Sometimes we would get into water fights and splash too much water on the floor. The next day our nurses would punish us by making us take our baths separately. Every night after my bath Anna would rock me in her lap and read the Bible to me. Sometimes she would tuck me in the canopied mahogany bed and read to me until I fell asleep.

On Saturdays the nurses got the day off. If we got tired of playing we would go to their quarters in the back of the house and sit, watching with fascination as they went through the ritual of dressing their hair. They would put a curling iron and a metal comb on a hot plate. Then they greased their hair with White Rose petroleum jelly. When the combs and iron got hot enough, they would straighten their hair with the comb and curl it with the iron. The beauty treatment took most of the day, and I could always tell when it was Saturday by the smell of hot grease all through the house.

In the summertime when school was out, Anna would take

us for long walks in the afternoon, sometimes stopping to visit with a Negro woman who walked through the neighborhood balancing a basket of fresh vegetables on her head. The woman would barter her produce in a singsong, chanting, "Buy yo' nize fresh turnip greens, right heyah!" If we were lucky, we would come across the Popsicle boy peddling his bike cart and ringing his bell. If we were double lucky, Anna would have remembered to ask Mother for some money.

One day when we were returning from an afternoon walk with Anna, we stopped to wait for a traffic light to change. As we stood on the street corner a car with two white men in it pulled up. They had the green light, but they didn't go. Instead they kept looking at us in a peculiar way.

Anna was scared. "Don't look at them men. Don't say nothing, just stand still."

They kept looking at us, and then one of them said, "How would you girls like to go for a ride?"

We had been told never to accept rides from strangers. We knew the man was doing wrong to ask us and we knew Anna was scared.

"You better go on and leave us alone," Anna said.

"We don't want a ride," we said.

Then one of them started to open his car door and come after us. Anna jerked at us and hollered, "Run home!"

We lit out, running with Anna behind us. We didn't stop until we reached the Mansion. We were crying and carrying on, and so was Anna. She told Mother what had happened. We described the car and Mother reported the incident to the local law-enforcement authorities.

Anna was kind, gentle and warm. She was so good to me I found it hard to believe she had ever done anything to harm anyone. One day I asked Mother what Anna had ever done that was so bad. She told me that Anna had been accused of murdering her mother's boyfriend. There had been no hard evidence against her. Her mother testified at the trial that Anna had stabbed the man in the ear with an ice pick. Anna maintained her innocence but when she was asked who committed the crime she remained silent.

When I heard the story I was more convinced than ever

that Anna was innocent. I didn't believe a mother would testify against her own child. It seemed more natural to me for the mother to have tried to take the blame and free her child. If Anna had committed the murder, she could have accused her mother, but she didn't.

When I told Mother that I didn't think Anna was guilty, she said, "That's what they all say." But I always believed Anna was innocent. When she finally got her parole and went back to her hometown, I cried and cried. I kept up with her for a while after she left; then she moved to another town and I never heard from her again.

The prison system was a very important part of life at the Mansion. It literally sustained the Mansion, not only by supplying household help but by furnishing needed commodities such as meat, vegetables, milk and fresh flowers. These services enabled the residents of the executive home to live and entertain in a lavish manner at a minimal cost to the taxpayers.

The entire male inmate population was housed in Kilby Prison, which was situated on a 3,000-acre farm on the outskirts of Montgomery. The prison guards rode horseback with their shotguns across their arms while the inmates worked in the fields. The crops were healthy and the yield was always high. The vegetables were used to feed the inmates and the prison wardens, who lived in white row houses just outside the high white brick walls. A special delivery of fresh vegetables was made to the Governor's Mansion daily during the season. The surplus crops of cotton and corn were sold at markets to help the prison system. Corn shucks were sold to businesses in New Mexico and Arizona for making hot tamales.

There was a large, rambling, white frame building with creaky wooden floors outside the prison walls where the wardens and guards took their lunch. The prison trusties cooked the food and served it up in bowls and platters and placed them on a large table with hot homemade rolls and corn bread. Occasionally, Mother took us out to Kilby for lunch with the wardens during the summer when the fresh vegetables were at their prime. For some reason vegetables were always tastier at Kilby than they were at the Mansion, and Mother was forever threatening to have the cooks assigned to work for her. In addition to raising vegetables, the prisoners bred and butchered cattle. They also maintained a fine dairy farm and furnished their own milk. They kept a few goats and, along with the cow's milk, brought fresh goat's milk to the Mansion to satisfy Governor Folsom's taste. The smell was a little odd, but the taste was a refreshing change.

One reason—besides the management—that the dairy enjoyed such a fine reputation was the prize bull that serviced the cows. The state had purchased the blue-ribbon bull because of his pedigree. That animal was the subject of many sight-seeing tours which we made, like trips to the zoo. Sometimes we brought our friends along to see this candidate for the *Guinness Book of World Records*.

It seemed appropriate that Alabama should have a super-sized bull since the state had a supersized Governor. Uncle Jimmy took unusual pride in quoting the animal's vital statistics. He was so large and strong that he was locked in an all-iron-bar cell, and a brass ring had been permanently placed in his nose to enable the dairy men to move him from place to place. What was especially interesting and educational for us children was that the bull was so valuable he was not allowed to pasture with the cows. The cows instead were bred by artificial insemination, a procedure initiated at the state prison in 1947 by Auburn University.

Besides housing the bull and the milking machines, the dairy barns also housed the horses on which the guards rode when they supervised the inmates in the fields. When the crops were not being harvested, we children were allowed to ride the horses for pleasure. One day Rachel and I were headed back to the barn after a nice uneventful ride. It was late in the afternoon and I guess the horses were hungry, because suddenly they broke into a run. The reins on my horse were not knotted together, Western style, and when I grabbed for the saddle to keep from falling off I dropped the reins.

I knew I was in trouble because the dirt road we were on went past the barn straight onto a busy highway. Without the reins I couldn't turn the horse into the barn and I certainly couldn't stop him. I knew if that horse went out on that highway the chances were good that I would be hit by a truck. I couldn't decide whether or not to jump off, so I screamed, but the horse kept up his racetrack gait.

When we reached the crest of the hill we passed the barn and headed straight toward the highway. I held on and closed my eyes. Suddenly the horse reared and stopped. When I opened my eyes I discovered three convicts holding hands, standing across the road, blocking the path of the runaway horse. I knew the horse could have plowed right through those men. They knew it, too, but they took the risk just the same. I felt very grateful to the convicts for saving my life, and the prison officials showed their appreciation by giving the inmates some time off their sentences.

Being a member of the official first family brought some changes in our lives. My father accepted a position with the highway department as a bridge engineer, which was a remarkable accomplishment, considering the fact that he acquired his engineering skills on the job rather than in the classroom. That put an end, once and for all, to the formerly mandatory life style of moving from town to town.

Daddy was a perfectionist who was as neat and organized in his personal habits as he was with a T-square and a drawing board, and although he was cast in the midst of a political whirlwind, he never succumbed to the popular theory, "It's not what you know, but who you know, that counts." Mother, however, did subscribe to that belief and in the early days of my father's career she did not hesitate to inform Daddy's superiors of the fact that her husband had the qualifications to be promoted when there was an opening. She was tactful and discreet, and Daddy never knew she ever spoke a word in his behalf. This is not to say there is any evidence that Mother was directly or indirectly responsible for Daddy's success. If she had opened every available door, every one would have slammed in Daddy's face if he had not had the ability—you just can't fake engineering skill. Daddy's colleagues were known to have said, "If I had my ambition and Charlie's engineering ability, I could go places." Daddy was conscientious, serious and inhibited. Mother was gregarious, assertive and ambitious. They had a combination of attributes that, in harmony, could have sounded a fine symphony but, if out of tune, could produce great discord.

Daddy took the Masonic degrees. The only prerequisites for

joining were good character and a belief in God. All I knew at the time was that he occasionally went to a secret meeting. I found it difficult to understand why he wouldn't tell me anything about his club. He would just wink and smile and say he was going to "ride the billy goat," which I thought would be fun for me, but I considered it a little inappropriate for a grown man to engage in such juvenile activities.

It was Mother's desire to have the children present when Uncle Jimmy made his maiden speech to the Legislature. She secured permission for Charles, Rachel, Melissa and me to be excused from classes that day. Charles was in the third grade in public school.

The schoolteachers had become angry at the Folsom administration over some education program. Charles, upon returning to class, was called upon to relate his experiences during his absence. He was reluctant to respond because Mother had a strict rule which forbade any personal and political gossip away from the Mansion. Upon failing to answer the teacher's inquiry, Charles was given a verbal dressing down. He began experiencing migraine headaches as a result of his embarrassment and humiliation. On the advice of Dr. Alice Hill Pye, a pediatrician, Mother transferred Charles to Hertz Military Academy. The move proved a boon to Charles's athletic and educational endeavors. He won a trophy for friendliness, cooperation and athletic achievements, and his grades placed him on the honor roll.

On weekends Charles went on hunting trips arranged by the Conservation Department. On a particular deer hunt he came back without a deer but brought home the carcass of a bobcat he had felled with a pistol as it crouched on a limb under which he was about to walk. He had the bobcat mounted and hung it on the wall in his room. After Charles took a course in taxidermy he soon had a stuffed owl, fox, squirrel and rattlesnake sharing his room.

One year the Conservation Officer brought us two motherless fawns he had found in the woods. We bottle-fed them until they were old enough to survive on their own and they were returned to the forest.

Melissa was four years old when we moved to Montgomery. She was the baby of the family. She was sweet and pretty and had as many curls as Shirley Temple. She had a happy disposition and was a delight to all of us. Melissa had been only sixteen months old when her mother died, and we all adored her and made over her, hoping to make up for the loss. Her birthday fell at the wrong time of the year for her to be admitted to first grade in public school, so Mother enrolled her in Miss Margaret Booth's private school when she was five.

Rachel was seven years old and I was eight when we moved to Montgomery. I was six months Rachel's senior, but we had started school the same year and we were in the same grade, although sometimes the teachers would not allow us to be in the same class. Rachel and I continued our education in the public school system. Midterm of second grade we entered Sayre Street School, which was near the home of Judge Sayre, former Justice of the Alabama Supreme Court and father of Zelda Sayre Fitzgerald.

Rachel and I were in the third grade in 1948, the year Zelda returned home for a respite from an Asheville, North Carolina, hospital where she had been under psychiatric care. Even though the teachers put their heads together in furtive discussions of the much-publicized escapades of Zelda and Scott Fitzgerald, we were much too young to grasp the significance of the subject of their whispers. Sometimes we interrupted our fun and games on the playground to watch the famous lady our teachers were so curious about as she passed our school on her brief outings. Still, we didn't realize our eyes had fallen on a tragic romantic heroine. Since we had not been exposed to the written works of Scott Fitzgerald, we could not yet appreciate the fact that this lady was the wife of a literary genius and a thinly disguised character in his books.

At first Rachel and I were sent to school in a black Cadillac limousine driven by the chauffeur, Winston Craig. Winston considered this mission beneath his dignity since he fancied himself the Governor's exclusive driver. He voiced his displeasure to Mother at home and to us on the way to school. Mother ignored him, but Rachel, who was predisposed to an ill temper, decided not to tolerate Winston's complaints. Taking matters into her own hands one day, she jumped out of the limousine and announced that she would walk to school.

She got to school all right, but it was Baldwin Junior High

instead of Sayre Street. When the principal found her wandering around the halls he asked her, "Don't you think you should go to school, young lady?"

Rachel replied, "I am going, if I can ever find my way."

Mother still refused to let Winston off the hook. Finally we convinced Mother that we were slowly but surely becoming unpopular with the other children and if she didn't allow us to walk to school we would soon be without a friend to our name. She gave us a few supervised trial runs and finally determined we were responsible enough to be trusted to make it on our own. Winston was much nicer to us and we were much happier. We met our friends on the way to school and played sidewalk games. We played hopscotch on the hexagonal cement stones. Another was one we made up. We would kick one of our penny loafers as far as we could, then walk in our stocking feet to the shoe, counting the stones as we went. The one whose shoe landed farthest away always won the game.

Mother believed strongly in developing a child's talents. So two afternoons a week we took piano lessons and the other three days we were instructed in tap dancing, ballet and acrobatics at Billy Pinkston's Studio.

When Mother planned her first big party for the Legislature, she decided we had had enough training to entertain for it. Besides his dance school, Billy Pinkston played the piano and led a swing band. Mother hired him to furnish the music and also the magic that would turn her three little girls into seasoned amateur performers overnight.

Mother decided to have an early evening garden party. The buffet tables lined both sides of the lawn behind the Governor's Mansion. Fresh seafood from the Alabama Gulf Coast was sent up especially for the affair. Ice carvings were on the tables. Shrimp, oysters, crabs and a variety of fish were prepared in an infinite variety of ways. Every conceivable food product found in Alabama was offered to tempt the palates of the lawmakers. Bourbon was served before dinner (in those days, if you asked a Southern gentleman if he would like some Scotch, he would have thought you meant the tape) and champagne was served after dinner.

The five hundred guests arrived, the ladies in evening

dresses and the men in tuxedos and black ties. Rachel and Melissa and I dressed for our debut in cowgirl suits with genuine leather and sheep's-wool chaps that Mother had brought from a trip out West. We had rehearsed our song and dance number for weeks.

After dinner was served we were given our cue to mount the stage and take our places in front of the band. Rachel and Melissa had talked about not even doing the show from the very first. I had been excited about the new experience and I did everything I could think of to keep my cousins from dropping out of the chorus line. Once on the stage, however, I developed a case of jitters so bad that my knees knocked. Rachel and Melissa seemed oblivious to the fact that anyone was around.

We did a song and dance number that went like this:

I'm an old cowhand from the Rio Grande,
But my legs ain't bowed [at which point we bowed our
    legs] and my cheeks [then we touched our cheeks with
    our fingers] ain't tan.
I'm a cowboy who never saw a cow,
Never roped a steer 'cause I don't know how,
Sho ain't fixin' to start in now.
Yippy—i—o—i—yay.

We were a big hit and Mother was gaining a reputation for being an outstanding hostess.

Chapter 12

RIDING IN A PARADE soon after he was elected governor, Jim Folsom turned to Nana Thomas, who was Alabama's Democratic Committeewoman at the time, and asked, "Do you think I'll ever be able to fulfill all the promises I've made to the people?"

Jim Folsom's efforts to make good his campaign pledges caused the most extended row between a governor and a legislature the state of Alabama has ever known. In describing his first administration, Big Jim would say, "I was elected Governor and I had a four-year fight with the Legislature."

The constitution of the state of Alabama requires the Legislature to assemble once every two years. The Legislature may convene for an unlimited number of additional sessions, but only by special call of the Governor. During his years as Chief Executive of Alabama, Jim Folsom called forty special sessions of the Legislature. Historically, that is the greatest number of special sessions of the Alabama Legislature ever called by any governor. The record documents the accuracy of Jim Folsom's own description of his tenure in office.

A group of legislators who were against the Folsom brand of politics formed a block in the Legislature, vowing to oppose every bill Folsom wanted passed. The Legislature completed its first regular session and adjourned without passing one proposal from the administration package. The lawmakers went home satisfied that they had whipped ole Big Jim. In actuality they had won only the first round in a fight that could go as many rounds as Jim Folsom chose. When Jim saw he couldn't beat his opposition in a vote count on the floor he decided he would wear them down with the executive power of the special call. Determined to get his programs passed, Uncle Jimmy called the Legislature right back into session, and they adjourned and went right back home.

The senators and representatives had just barely returned to their hometowns when Governor Folsom announced he was calling another special session. The body reassembled and adjourned, still without bending to the will of the Governor.

The legislators had barely gotten the home-county dust on their automobile tires when Governor Folsom sent out a call for yet another session. They returned once again. The legislators had just gotten their seats warmed when the anti-Folsom block voted to adjourn. They were meeting themselves coming and going between Montgomery and their hometowns.

The legislators were filled with obstinacy and Jim Folsom was full of determination. The two forces continued their head-on clash until finally the members of both houses, realizing they faced the very real prospects of spending every day of the next four years in Montgomery, passed the Governor's bills and went home.

This was a frustrating period in the life of Jim Folsom. It was during this trying time that he found an ally in a twenty-seven-year-old freshman representative from Barbour County named George Corley Wallace.

George Wallace did not approve of the tactics of the legislative block, and although he had not supported Jim Folsom in his bid for the governorship, the young activist voted with the Folsom forces on many bills. George Wallace, like Jim Folsom, was a populist. He and Folsom found a common ground in the common good of the people, which is not too surprising when you analyze the backgrounds of the two men. Both were born and reared in rural counties in south Alabama. They were familiar with the needs of the farmer. Both their fathers and grandfathers had been active in county politics and had held public office all their lives. The young men had been exposed to an environment of political discussions and debates. At an early age they both aspired to become governor of their state. Their ambitions were fired by a burning desire to improve the life of the people around them. The chief parallel in the lives of George Wallace and James Folsom that probably shaped their destinies and gave them the impetus to become governor, when other men with similar backgrounds did not, was the fact that both of their fathers had died by the time the boys were eighteen years old.

During the years he was governor, Jim Folsom saw the passage of populist legislation that would upgrade the lives of Alabamians for generations to come. The program included a salary raise for schoolteachers, an increase in old-age pension checks, additional funds for the blind and disabled and for tubercular patients, removal of the poll tax, funds for the farm-to-market roads and a bond issue for highway expansion.

The most monumental bill passed was the Wallace Trade School Act. George Wallace sponsored the bill and Governor Folsom signed it into law.

When the time came to name the first trade school and select the building, Governor Folsom called in his friend George Wallace.

"George, where do you think that school ought to be built?" Uncle Jimmy said.

"Governor, it would help me a lot with the people down my way if you'd build it in south Alabama."

"There's more industry in north Alabama. I'm half a mind to build it up there."

"Governor, I know it's a little early to be speculating, but I figure you'll be wanting to run for another term. I'm prepared to pledge my support to you the next time you run if you'll build that school in my district."

"I've got to build four more trade schools. I can put one of the others in north Alabama. I suppose I could put the first one in Dothan. That's not in your county, George, but that's the biggest town near you and it would service the people in your area."

"A school in Dothan would take care of the whole southeastern part of the state."

"You know I'm chairman of the Board of Education. I'll

have to meet with the members and tell them what I want to name the school. I wish I could name it after you, George, but you know the law won't allow me to name a public building after anybody who's living. You got any suggestions?"

"Yes, sir, when I was a boy my father used to talk about how trade schools would help Alabama. I'd appreciate it if you could see fit to name the school after him."

"I'll tell the board to build the school at Dotham, and we'll name it the George Wallace, Sr., Trade School."

"Thank you, Governor."

"By the way, George, somebody told me you wanted that appointment to the board of Tuskegee Institute. Is that right?"

"Yes, sir, Governor."

"If you want it, you can have it. I'll have my office issue a statement to the press announcing your appointment today. That's the finest Negro college in the United States. I'd like for it to stay on that level."

"Yes, sir."

"I'm gonna hold you to that promise you made me, George. You'd make a good campaign manager for south Alabama."

There was so much animosity among some of the legislators toward the new governor that a group of Folsom's strongest opponents formulated a plan to try to impeach him when he had been in office less than a year. Their method was to draw up a bill giving the Legislature the authority to call itself into session. Then they planned to call a special session of their own to consider impeachment. They passed the bill in both houses, as required by law. It was then presented to the people for a vote. The people voted it down, but only after Uncle Jimmy traveled the length and breadth of the state speaking out against it. That was the hardest campaign he ever waged. If the bill had passed it would have tilted the balance of governmental power toward the legislative branch.

Jim Folsom was a country boy who came to town intent on changing things. The old-timers resented him because he threatened the establishment. The Alabama Legislature had been controlled by a handful of senators for years. They knew Jim

Folsom wanted to reapportion the Legislature. With reapportionment many of them would lose their seats. When the legislators saw that the people supported their governor, the impeachment plan died.

Political discussions were hot and heavy in those days. Talk of the battles in the Legislature flowed freely around the Mansion and the adults in our family did not subdue their conversations in the presence of children. At some point in every discussion the name of George Wallace would surface. It was a name that was spoken in a tone of approval and promise of better things to come. The name of George Wallace was as familiar to me as any household word is to any other youngster.

Uncle Jimmy had a clearly defined sense of protocol. At first I interpreted this as the natural goodness of the man, but I later realized he had a genuine knowledge of what was proper in official situations. He continued his grand style of entertaining and was adamant about leaving the names of the warring tribesmen of the Legislature on the invitation list.

I remember vividly one social affair when the senators and representatives were invited. Mother thought the hour was too late and decided that the children would not be allowed to come down for this particular party. Customarily we were allowed to mingle with the guests and at the very least make a brief appearance. I suppose that is one reason this occasion stands out in my memory.

Following Mother's instructions, the maids had bathed and dressed Rachel, Melissa and me in our nightgowns long before the first guest arrived. Because we were forbidden to go downstairs we imagined that something would be going on that we should not see, hear or tell. Of course that aroused our curiosity to uncontrollable heights. As the guests began arriving we positioned ourselves on the staircase and peeped through the spindles. The longer we went unnoticed, the braver we became and the farther down the steps we descended. We were almost at the first landing when a young couple followed the butler to a coat closet under the staircase. As they removed their wraps, one of them saw us crouched behind the banister. They smiled and waved and we giggled and ran up the stairs. We peeped over the banister and the man and lady were still looking up after us.

"Come down so we can see you," the lady said as she motioned to us.

"We can't. Mother won't let us," I said.

"Can we come up and see you?" the man said.

"I guess so," I said.

They both came up the steps to where we were hiding. "You are three mighty pretty little girls," the lady said. Then she picked us up one by one and kissed us.

The man said, "And I'll bet you'll be even prettier when you grow up," and he patted each of us on the head. "Now tell us your names."

"This is Rachel, this is Melissa and I'm Cornelia," I answered, pointing to each cousin and then to myself. "Who are you?"

The man answered, "This is my wife, Lurleen, and I'm George Wallace."

"Don't tell Mother you saw us," I said.

"We promise we won't tell a soul," they agreed.

Whenever the Legislature took a recess for the weekend, Uncle Jimmy would go to his office on Saturday mornings to read his mail and sign whatever bills had been passed. No matter how busy he was he never was so occupied that he forgot to spend some time with us children. He would treat us to a milkshake in the Capitol cafeteria and then we would play on the Confederate monument on the Capitol grounds while Uncle Jimmy finished up his business.

One Sunday, not long after we moved to Montgomery, Mother told us we were old enough to join the church. I didn't really understand what she meant. I probably thought I was already a member, since I had been going to church all my life.

I had started attending church before I could walk. On my first outing I was taken to the First Baptist Church in Elba. Mother enrolled me in the Cradle Roll Department. I still have the aging, yellowed certificate given when I graduated to the Primary Department. That piece of paper would be worthless to anyone else, but it has more value to me than all the stock certificates in the world, and more meaning than the two honorary doctorates I received after George was shot. I consider those two degrees significant because they tell more about the quality of life I've lived than the grades I made on a report card. The reason I value the Cradle Roll Certificate more than the two honorary doctorates is that I believe I received the latter because of the former.

Mother told us the preacher would talk to us before we were baptized. He did and I understood perfectly what baptism was all about. My heart was in the right place—it was open to receive—and although the whole thing had been Mother's idea, after my talk with the preacher I very much wanted to profess Jesus Christ as my Savior. On Easter Sunday, April 17, 1949, we were baptized at the First Baptist Church.

Every Sunday morning we attended Sunday school and church. Sometimes we went on family picnics out in the country. If we ate at the Mansion, after lunch Uncle Jimmy would sit and read his paper on the front porch in his undershirt and khakis with his bare feet propped on the railing.

One Sunday after he finished reading his paper he threw on a casual shirt and his walking shoes and called Rachel, Melissa and me from our play in the front yard to take a walk down the street with him. We walked three blocks south of the Mansion on Perry Street, where he paused in front of a beautiful white-columned mansion belonging to Mrs. Ligon, who was the widow of General Ligon, a former lieutenant governor of Alabama. Indisputably the Ligon home was the finest and most beautiful in Montgomery. A Greek revival structure, it was the kind of dwelling people expected to see in the old romantic South. It gave the feeling of the glory and splendor of *Gone With the Wind* without the tragedy one associates with memories of Tara.

Life magazine had just published an article featuring the ten most beautiful capitol buildings and governors' mansions in the nation. Alabama's Capitol, according to the report, was the most beautiful, while the Governor's Mansion was listed as the ugliest in the land.

"How would y'all like to live here?" Uncle Jimmy asked.

"I think it would make a beautiful Governor's Mansion," I answered.

"Let's take a look inside," Uncle Jimmy said, as he rang the doorbell. A butler opened the door and invited us in. His name was Buster. He served us some lemonade and told Uncle Jimmy that Mrs. Ligon, who owned the house, was away in Europe.

All the furniture was hidden under white covers to protect it from dust, which indicated that Mrs. Ligon would be away for a month or longer. The pieces looked like odd-shaped ghost figures to me and would have created a spooky atmosphere except for Buster's warm, friendly manner toward us. The floor plan of the house was not much different from the Governor's Mansion except that the massive staircase faced the front door, rather than being to the left of the entrance foyer. The light-colored floors were bordered in an intricate design with inlaid strips of darker wood. The ceilings were trimmed with ornate molding. There was a sun porch with a tile floor and ceiling fans; it was enclosed on three sides by glass-paneled sections that could be removed in the summer.

One of the outstanding features of the house was the gold-leaf mirrors that had been imported from Europe. It seemed as if the house was built around them, because they fit perfectly up into the curve of the ceiling. Two of the shorter mirrors were hung over the fireplaces. Two tall floor-to-ceiling pier mirrors faced each other on opposite walls of the large drawing room. If you stood in between them your image was reflected into infinity. There was a mosaic tile design on the porch in front of the door. All the rooms on the first floor had French doors that opened onto the white-marbled terrace porch that surrounded the house.

The detail of the Ligon home was more elaborate than the Governor's Mansion and the house was more suitable for entertaining.

As we left, Uncle Jimmy turned to the butler. "Buster, you tell Mrs. Ligon to call me when she gets back home. I want to talk to her about buying this house."

"I don't believe she wants to sell her house, Governor Folsom, but I'll sho' tell her you wants to talk to her about it," Buster said.

When Mrs. Ligon returned to Montgomery she had dinner

with the Governor and shortly afterward the papers were signed finalizing the purchase of the Ligon home for the Executive Mansion of Alabama. The newspapers were critical of the purchase. Uncle Jimmy countered by saying he intended to live there in four years, which was tantamount to announcing that, although he couldn't succeed himself, he planned to run for another term as governor four years later.

Becoming the youngest governor in the United States, besides giving Uncle Jimmy a place in history, also made him famous. His size and his flamboyant personality made him colorful. He was young, handsome and, to top it off, he was a widower. He was named as one of the ten most eligible bachelors in America. That makes for good copy in anybody's magazine.

Life magazine sent some of its people down to Alabama to do a story. The writer in the group must have thought he had climbed Jack's beanstalk by mistake. I guess he must have believed the entire Southland was inhabited by a race of giants because when he took one look at Big Jim he asked, "How do they grow 'em so big down here?" And offering his own explanation, he added inquisitively, "Put fertilizer in your shoes?"

After the *Life* magazine story appeared in print, Uncle Jimmy's movements were followed closely by the press. The publicity also enlarged his following of female admirers. Before long he was so well known that when he made a trip to New York the women mobbed him just the way they mob Elvis Presley. If they couldn't have him to keep, they would settle for a kiss to remember him by. And kiss them he did, one and all.

It was a new switch for a politician to kiss pretty women instead of babies and the public reacted favorably to the new image. The reporters ate it up and they wrote it up. Pretty soon, while Governor Folsom was still called "Big Jim" in Alabama, the rest of the world knew him as "Kissin' Jim," and when I say the rest of the world that's not an exaggeration. I was amazed when I toured Australia years later and a German-Jew refugee who discovered I was from Alabama asked me to tell him about "Kissin' Jim Folsom." Of course the first thing I told him, much to his astonishment and delight, was that "Kissin' Jim" just happened to be my uncle.

The more publicity Uncle Jimmy got, the more sought after he was by the ladies. The telephone rang off the hook at the Mansion, all hours of the day and night. Most of the women who called were strangers; many were anonymous. Mother got stuck with the calls. In her mind, Mother had already made a match for her famous brother. She had accompanied him on a trip to Salt Lake City, Utah, to the National Governors' Conference in the summer of 1947. In attendance was the Governor of California, Earl Warren, who later became Chief Justice of the United States Supreme Court. With him was his beautiful blond daughter, Virginia. Uncle Jimmy escorted Virginia and her sister to dinner. Mother was convinced that Virginia would be the perfect match for a young man making his mark on the political scene; Virginia had exhibited more than a passing interest in the handsome Southern governor. By all calculations it would have been a good pairing, but the distance between California and Alabama proved too great for a romance to bloom.

Times were good. Life was rich and full. Summer was the best time of year to me. The highlight of the summer was the annual trip to Gulf Shores, Alabama, eighteen miles of sugar-white sand beaches on the Gulf of Mexico, which is all we have left from Alabama's selling the panhandle (which includes Pensacola and Panama City) to Florida. Most Alabama governors take their vacations there to help promote the beaches. The state owned a row of cabins around a lake in eyesight of the beach. Cabins 15 and 16 were reserved for us for two weeks every summer. We loaded up two station wagons with food and fishing gear and several cases of RC (Royal Crown) Cola and Nehi orange and grape that were sent to us by John and Iva Cooper. (They were our back-door neighbors in Cullman and they owned a bottling plant. Out of loyalty to John and Iva, we never had Cokes in the Mansion.)

Charles was allowed to take a small boat with a 12-hp motor out alone to fish. We crabbed every day off the pier in front of the cabin. We'd tie a fishhead onto a pier and drop it into the water. When the line moved out away from the pier we'd know a crab was trying to take our bait. Slowly we'd pull the strings up and when the crab was almost to the surface we'd dip him up with a long-handled net. Catching fifty or a hundred a day was ordinary. Mother was proud of our catch because that meant she could make crab gumbo.

Gulf Shores was near Mobile, the shipping port of Alabama. Since the state operated the docks, a 100-foot yacht which was appropriately named *The Dixie* was kept available for the governor to entertain industrial prospects. The captain would bring the yacht over while we were at the beach and would take us on overnight cruises. We usually went into the Alabama bayous where the shrimp boats moored, or around the oyster beds in Mobile Bay. There was a Cajun cook from Louisiana on board. The seafood dishes he cooked were out of this world. The captain loved having children aboard and let each of us take a turn at the wheel. The tendency of most people is to oversteer the boat, making it take wide swings to the right or left of the intended course. The trick is to make small adjustments. The other children didn't get the knack of it, but I did, and I would steer for as long as the captain would allow. I quickly became his favorite "first mate."

We were usually vacationing at Gulf Shores over the Labor Day weekend, when the local people put on their annual barbecue picnic at the state park. There were boat races, a beauty contest and a watermelon-eating contest. Uncle Jimmy would make a speech and crown the beauty queen. Naturally he would give the girl a kiss as he placed the crown on her head.

By some people's standards, I suppose you could say we lived like millionaires. We lived in a mansion with plenty of servants, rode in a chauffeur-driven limousine and had a yacht available to us. The luxurious life-style did not turn us into snobs. We knew the good life we were enjoying was there because the people voted for Uncle Jimmy—not for any other reason. And we never forgot it. None of us got the big head because we were kin to the Governor; our elders never gave us a chance. They constantly reminded us to be nice to people.

That wasn't a hard assignment. When people are nice to you it's easy to be nice back, and everybody was good to us. People were always sending us gifts and doing nice things for us. Unlike the wealthy, who have to pay through their teeth because everyone knows they have money, we were never charged a penny in many places we went. Of course, we paid for clothes and things that were purchased at a store, but we rarely paid an admission to sporting events, cultural events, fairs, rodeos, horse shows and so on. The theater managers sent us yearly passes to the movies, some restaurant owners refused to let us pay the bill, and a few doctors never billed us at all. The good life we led wouldn't have been nearly as good without the many kindnesses shown to us by a lot of good folks.

There were other special privileges we enjoyed because of Uncle Jimmy being governor. One was meeting the famous people who came to Alabama. The biggest thrill for me was meeting Gene Autry, who had come to headline a rodeo. He was the singing cowboy film star of my childhood. I had watched him on the screen every Saturday. Seeing him in real life, for a little girl eight years old, was too good to be true. I also had the pleasure of meeting Johnny Mack Brown (another favorite Western movie star) when he came back to his hometown of Dothan, Alabama, to preside over the Peanut Festival. Another celebrity I met who had a special appeal to me as a child was Emmett Kelly, the internationally famous "sad" clown of the Ringling Brothers Circus. Charles had a special treat when Babe Ruth came to Montgomery to play an exhibition baseball game. After the game Babe Ruth autographed a baseball and handed it to Charles. Baseball was big in those days and it was Daddy's favorite spectator sport.

Most of the notables who came into Montgomery found their way to the Capitol or the Governor's Mansion. Some of the ones we entertained were Lily Pons and Helen Traubel, of operatic fame; Roy Acuff, the "Wabash Cannon Ball" of the Grand Ol' Opry; actress Diana Barrymore; and Eddy Arnold. Roy Acuff later became my employer and Eddy Arnold tried unsuccessfully to buy my Martin guitar.

Constance Bennett at the height of her movie career came to Montgomery to join her husband, who was stationed at Maxwell Air Force Base. The first thing she said when she arrived was, "I'm looking forward to a kiss from Governor Folsom."

The most legendary figure to visit the Governor's Mansion was Hank Williams. I remember the time I saw him there. He was wearing a white Western suit, a white Western hat and cowboy boots. He played his guitar and sang, then autographed some pictures for us. Hank was riding the crest of success as a country music singer and songwriter. His records "Lovesick Blues," "Your Cheatin' Heart," "Cold, Cold Heart" and "Hey, Good Lookin'" were smash hits. He was drawing sellout crowds everywhere he appeared.

Hank was well known in Alabama before he left Montgomery and went to Nashville and made the big time. Lots of folks had watched him grow up and had recognized his talent and encouraged him to go all the way. One of Hank's fans from his youth was my uncle Ross Clark, Aunt Thelma's husband. Uncle Ross had been a district manager for the Federal Seed Loan Office and covered the area of Georgiana, where Hank lived as a boy. When Uncle Ross was working in the Georgiana office he would give Hank two dollars to play and sing for him.

Hank Williams was one of the few people who just dropped by the Mansion whenever he was passing by to talk old times. Some people got nervous when they came to the Governor's Mansion, but Mother said Hank was more at ease than anyone else who visited us. When Hank died, in January of 1953, his body was brought back to Montgomery for burial, and 20,000 mourners jammed the streets the day of his funeral.

I was not old enough to understand Hank's music in those days, although I was crazy about the way he sang "Lovesick Blues." It was called hillbilly music, or tear-jerking. The people who liked it the most were people who had experienced in their own lives some of the sadness that Hank wrote about in his songs. After I suffered a few disappointments in my own life I gained a new appreciation for Hank's songs and all hillbilly music.

British nobility also visited the Mansion. Mother was alerted days ahead to prepare for a lord and lady from England. Wanting everything to be proper, Mother asked an older person in town to instruct Charles how to bow and Rachel, Melissa and me how to curtsy. We practiced several afternoons before the couple's scheduled visit. It was a good thing I did, because the first time I held my skirt out with both hands and crossed one leg behind the other I lost my balance and fell over. (Try it, if you haven't lately.)

In the middle of our practice session one afternoon Uncle Jimmy came home from the office. He passed us in the upstairs living room and did a double take. Then he started hollering for Mother.

"Ruby, what in the world have you got these children doing?"

Mother explained that she was trying to teach us the correct way to greet a lord and lady.

"I don't want my chil'un bowing and scraping to royalty," he bellowed.

"I didn't want you to be embarrassed," Mother said as she tried to shrink out of range of his powerful voice.

"Good gracious, woman, don't you know America was founded to escape the tyranny of the Crown?" he shouted, as if she should have thought of it before he reminded her.

Mother didn't try to answer that one.

Mother was not in the habit of defying her brother's wishes. It just so happened that Uncle Jimmy wasn't in the room when we were introduced to the distinguished guests, so we girls curtsied and Charles bowed and we hurried upstairs, hoping we would not catch the wrath of our patriotic uncle.

Political figures came to Montgomery, too. The most famous was Harry Truman. He was already President, having inherited the office upon the death of Franklin Delano Roosevelt. Truman had received the presidential nomination from the Democratic Party at the 1958 convention. Alabama was one of several Southern states that bolted the party at the convention. They formed the Dixiecrat Party and nominated Strom Thurmond as their presidential candidate. The Republicans ran Thomas Dewey. Uncle Jimmy was loyal to the Democratic Party and pledged his support to the party nominee, much to the consternation of many of his constituents and colleagues. Since Governor Folsom was the only Southern governor who endorsed the Truman ticket, Montgomery was scheduled on the whistle-stop train tour the Truman campaign was making through the country. When the train pulled into Union Station, Uncle Jimmy headed the welcoming party that greeted Mr.

Truman. Then, in November, Harry Truman was elected President of the United States in his own right.

Opinion holds that a prominent public figure has little or no private life. While the adage is generally true, Uncle Jimmy kept a part of his personal life from public scrutiny and family censorship. Scrupulously avowing his fondness for the feminine gender, he adeptly concealed the identity of his true love. He revealed the object of his affection to followers and family alike by unexpectedly walking across the Mansion threshhold one day with his bride in his arms.

The girl who had captured the biggest heart in the state—literally and figuratively—was a five-foot-two-inch, black-haired, brown-eyed, nineteen-year-old beauty named Jamelle Moore. Uncle Jimmy's philosophy about marriage was as folksy as his politics. He said, "The way to keep a woman in the home is to keep her barefooted and pregnant." He preached it and he practiced it. No Women's Liberation darling was he, even though he appointed the first woman judge to the Alabama State Court of Criminal Appeals.

The marriage produced seven beautiful children. Rachel and Melissa made nine altogether. Uncle Jimmy failed to keep Jamelle shoeless and insisted that she travel with him constantly, leaving her home only long enough to give birth to their children. In proper First Lady fashion she looked beautiful through it all and never lost her smile in public or private life.

My elation over my uncle's marriage was short-lived. My excitement and joy in welcoming a new member into our family was soon replaced by the revelation that our household was about to disintegrate. The idea had never occurred to me that Uncle Jimmy's marriage would cause me to be separated from Rachel and Melissa, who had become like sisters to me, and Uncle Jimmy, who had been like a father to me. Happy with the way things were, I failed to comprehend the need to change our fairy-tale existence, even given Mother's full explanation.

I was floating in a sea of confusion soon to be engulfed by an emotional typhoon. The trauma of the first experience had not subsided before my young psyche was dealt an even more severe blow. Shortly after we left the Mansion my mother and daddy ended their marriage of seventeen years.

My parents' divorce was a very painful episode in my life, compounded by the loss of my cousins and uncle. Divorce has a way of leaving a void in the lives of the children affected. There is an ever-present yearning for the absent parent and hours spent weaving fantasies of children and parents happily reunited. At first it was difficult for me to accept and understand my parents' differences. I was hurting so much inside I only felt that if they loved me they should reconcile their disagreements and put an end to my suffering.

When I became older and learned to respect my parents as adults and appreciate their differences, I was amazed that their marriage survived as long as it did. I was glad that my parents had not tried to rear me in an unpleasant atmosphere of resentment, indifference and dishonesty. There were no fights over custody, visitation or money. What helped me accept the reality of the situation was the consistent love and support I received from both my parents.

Chapter 13

WE WERE EXILED to Elba—not quite an island but almost encircled by Pea River. The levee around town is a visual reminder of the 1929 flood that caused the evacuation of the townspeople, took some lives and left others homeless. The town survived the flood and the people developed a strength of character and a faith in God molded by living through and overcoming their common tragedy.

In the middle of town sits the Coffee County courthouse. Stores face four streets around the square. One corner of the square exhibits the town's concrete goldfish pond and a public drinking fountain fed by a natural well with eternal flow with no pump, a symbol of the city of flowing wells. Artesian wells abound, supplying pure cool water to the 5,000 citizens and overflowing the city swimming pool in the summer.

My grandfather, Joshua Marion Folsom, had moved his family to Elba from his 600-acre farm at Tabernacle, six miles in the country. He maintained the farm, served as deputy sheriff to his brother, Frank Folsom, owned stock in the Elba Exchange Bank and was a county commissioner. Even after Grandpa Folsom moved to town he always sided with the country politicians against the courthouse crowd. Politics was a way of life with the Folsoms. There were seven children in the family: Fred, Thelma, Cecil, Robert, Carl, James and Ruby. Fred was a tax collector, Cecil a sheriff, Robert ran for mayor several times, James of course was Governor and Ruby once made a bid for Secretary of State.

Coming back to Elba was coming home. I had been born

in the front bedroom of my Grandmother Folsom's home. Mother endured the pain of natural childbirth assisted by Dr. Charles Hayes, the only doctor in town, and a black nurse, Ethel Anderson.

Mother likes to tell how Dr. Hayes described me. "She has hair as black as a crow with a million ringlets all over her head, her eyes are as blue as the sky and her skin as fair as a lily." Much to my mother's disappointment, my eyes turned brown before I was a year old. Ethel still laughs when she reminds Mother how mad she was at Daddy for causing her suffering, even though I don't think any mother ever wanted a baby more than my mother wanted me—and she wanted a girl!

Mother had the good sense to name me Marion after my Grandfather Folsom and Cornelia after my Grandmother Folsom. I loved my name and I grew up with much pride in the fact that I was the only grandchild who carried the names of both Grandpa and Grandma Folsom. My friends were never able to tag me with a nickname. One tried to call me "Corny" but never succeeded in making it stick. Every time she called, Mother would tell her no one by that name lived at our house. The only problem I ever had with being called Cornelia was that some people couldn't pronounce my name correctly. I would have to spell it C'nelia before I could get them to understand that in the South the *r* was silent.

The saddest thing about coming back to Elba was that my Grandmother Folsom was no longer with us. Granny had died in the spring of 1946 during Uncle Jimmy's campaign for governor.

Grandfather Folsom had died when my mother was six years old and Granny had reared her children by the Bible. She tried to instill them with Christian attitudes and even shaped their political philosophies. She counseled Uncle Jimmy about his political campaigns, advising him not to criticize his opponents. She told him, "When your political opponents sling mud at you, leave it alone, let it dry and it'll fall off by itself."

Found among Granny's personal effects were touching letters from Uncle Jimmy telling her about his renewed friendships with prominent politicians in Montgomery and Washington who had been friends of his deceased father. She encouraged and fostered his political ambitions.

The Folsom brothers and sisters at the Folsom farm: Uncle Fred, Auntie, Uncle Bob, Mother, Uncle Jimmy and Uncle Cecil.

My huge Uncle Jimmy and his wife, Jamelle,
with most of their huge family (two yet to come): Rachel,
Melissa, Jim, Jack, Bama, Scrappy and Josh.

If only Granny could have lived a few months longer she could have seen her son realize his political dream. How proud she would have been if she could have seen him on Inauguration Day.

Since my Grandfather Folsom died before I was born, I only knew him from the memories of others. He loved music and played the fiddle rather well. He fostered an intense dislike for the KKK. He respected Granny's wishes about not having liquor in the home. However, he did indulge in a nip when he was off with the men. During prohibition days he went on a fishing trip to Florida with some friends. One of them brought along some moonshine whiskey and Grandpa Folsom partook of the spirits. Several days later he died from lead poisoning.

After losing her husband, Granny took an even firmer stand against the evils of liquor. She started her campaign against spirits at home by asking each of her children to sign the family Bible with a solemn pledge that they would never touch a drop of whiskey. Only James and Ruby signed. Although Aunt Thelma's name does not appear in the Bible she never took a drink in her life, and after Granny passed away she took up the banner against whiskey and even became head of the Elba Temperance Committee.

I never heard anyone mention Granny's name without noting that she was a good Christian woman, not by reputation but by her acts and deeds and attitudes toward other people. She was generous and hospitable. The doors of her home were open to friends and strangers alike. Her children were told there would always be room at her table for one more and she never complained about how many mouths she had to feed. Mother is most like Granny in that way. I admired the legacy Granny left and hoped that because I bore her name I might have inherited some of the qualities that would enable me to become the kind of Christian she had been. I often thought that if people remembered me with the same kind words with which they revered Granny I would have truly lived a successful life.

Mother went home to Elba often while Daddy was moving about with his engineering jobs. This made it possible for me to spend many precious hours with Granny when I was a little girl. Her eyes were too weak to thread a needle, so I would thread her needles and then she would teach me to mend and darn. Sometimes I helped her sweep the backyard with a stick broom, something she seemed to do more to keep busy than out of need. My fondest memory was of sitting with Granny on the front porch swing singing hymns. She taught me to sing the first hymn I ever knew—her favorite—"Bringing in the Sheaves." Granny had a rose garden in the side yard. She tended it herself and soon after she died the rosebushes died, too.

We buried my grandmother near the Folsom family farm at Tabernacle Cemetery next to the graves of her husband, Joshua, and an infant son who had died.

A little later we buried Uncle Carl in the same family plot. Uncle Carl was the only one of Granny's children who had not married. He was a captain in the Army and was killed in the Philippines a few days after the end of World War II. We were living in Cullman when Mother received the telegram that her brother was dead. I heard Mother screaming and when I rushed to see what had happened to her, she was sprawled on the stairs, sobbing, with the crumpled yellow paper still clutched in her hand. I shared Mother's grief and sense of loss. I had been Uncle Carl's pet and I loved him very much. The last time I saw him he was passing through Elba with a military convoy. He pulled his jeep out of the line in front of Granny's house and rode me around the block before he left to go to war.

When we received notification of Uncle Carl's death, Granny had already had her first stroke. She had been in Cullman looking after Rachel and Melissa when she had become ill and had gone back to Elba. That's when we moved in with Uncle Jimmy. No one told Granny that Uncle Carl had been killed for fear the strain would cause her to have another stroke. They made excuses when she asked why Carl hadn't written lately. The deception became more difficult and the children suspected Granny had guessed the truth. They realized they would have to tell her before Uncle Carl's body was shipped home but they were spared that painful duty, as Granny died before Uncle Carl's coffin reached the States more than a year after he died.

Uncle Carl was given a full military funeral. All the Folsoms gathered for the second time in a year in the old cemetary next to the white, wooden Tabernacle Church. We sat on the country hillside staring through tear-blurred eyes at the American flag draped over the mahogany coffin while a rifle fired a last salute. There was silence; then a trumpet slowly played taps and from the distant woods another bugler faintly echoed each note until the last tone faded into nothingness. For the first time in my life I was experiencing the pain and sorrow brought about by war. I can't describe the depth of hurt I felt, nor can I explain it. Perhaps it was because—even though I was only eight years old—I recognized how unnecessary it is to lose precious human lives to senseless wars.

Granny and Uncle Carl were not there to greet me when I came home to Elba but Granny's house was still there and so were all the things that reminded me of the joy-filled days I had spent with her.

The big oak tree was still standing in front of the house, the scuppernong vine over the smokehouse had not stopped producing, the pecans still fell from the pecan tree in the backyard. The crepe myrtle and mimosa trees still made me sneeze. Granny's house was still cold in the winter and her handmade quilts and comforters still kept me warm at night. The kitchen food safe was still being used, as was the iron Franklin stove, but Granny's churn sat idle in the corner. Her hand-crocheted doilies were all about on the living-room tables. Nothing had changed much, not even the front porch swing—it still squeaked just the way it always had.

Mother's only sister, Thelma, and her husband, Ross Clark, were living in Granny's house. I always called them Auntie and Uncle Ross. They had moved back to Elba the year after the flood to help look after Granny since all the other children had married and left home.

Uncle Ross had built a log house on the lot adjoining the Folsom home. He had taken much pride in building the house and had finished it on the inside with plaster walls and hardwood floors. Daddy engineered the building of the columns and flower boxes across the front with miniature logs.

Mother, Charles and I moved into the log house and Auntie and Uncle Ross stayed in Granny's house. We actually split our time between the two houses.

Auntie was twenty years old when Mother was born and

had always helped look after her brothers and sister. She bossed everybody in the family—which was all right until they all grew up and decided they didn't want to be bossed any more. Auntie still told the Folsom brood what to do whenever she pleased, and more than once they told her to mind her own business. As Auntie said, "I always try to tell you what's right," and she did. Her favorite saying was, "Put first things first."

Auntie was very Victorian in her attitudes. Uncle Ross by contrast was a fun-loving, good-natured man. He was warm and affectionate and he loved Auntie to death. He called her "Sweet Gal."

The conflicts between their personalities were sometimes comical. One time when Uncle Ross was out of town he called Auntie to tell her he would be late getting home.

"Sweet Gal, this is Ross," he said.

"Have you been drinking?" Auntie snapped.

"Now what makes you think that?" Ross edged.

"Why, I can smell it over the phone!" Auntie declared.

If Auntie ever found a bottle hidden in the car or house she would bust it in the sink and let it run down the drainpipe.

Uncle Ross was always cheerful. He had a little bottle of brown liquid medicine that helped him sleep. He called it his "Good night, Irene" medicine. He would gulp down one teaspoon before he went to bed every night and sing a few bars of "Good Night, Irene" and fall sound asleep. In the mornings he'd do a sort of dance shuffle step around the house. While he shaved he would whistle and sing over and over, "A whistling woman and a crowing hen never come to no good end." I never understood that verse except that roosters crow, not hens!

Uncle Ross liked a full cup of coffee which he would saucer and blow until it was cool enough to drink. He loved raw oysters simmered in scalded milk drowned in pure butter and pepper. He often asked Auntie to prepare scrambled eggs and canned pork brains for his supper, a dish I found quite delectable once I ever got up the nerve to try it. Uncle Ross made a habit of making other people feel better. When he passed someone on the street and they would ask, "How ya feelin', Ross?" he'd always say, "The finest in the world."

The insurance company was paying off now and Uncle

Ross was president. He began looking for ways to invest his money. He bought some rental houses and a warehouse, built some stores downtown, bought some property in Florida and started a concrete-block business. Auntie found all this acceptable till she found he also had built the new pool hall across the street from the First Baptist Church. That was the maddest I ever saw Auntie—except for the time I left my color crayons on the floor after she told me repeatedly to pick them up and she got mad and threw them in the fireplace and they caught the roof on fire.

Auntie and Uncle Ross didn't have any children—not of their own—which was a blessing for those of us they showered with love and time and everything we needed. They helped raise Charles and me and most of Uncle Jimmy's children.

Uncle Ross thought Charles belonged to him—and vice versa. Charles was never happy living anywhere but Elba. The town was made for the boy and the boy for the town. After we moved to Elba Charles never lived anywhere else except when he went off to college.

Charles loved to hunt, as did all the men in our family. Uncle Ross and Charles hunted in season and shot skeet at the Troy Country Club out of season. When Uncle Ross bought Charles a new gun he gave me his old .22 rifle. At the beginning of every hunting season he would buy Charles a case of shotgun shells and give me $40, which was the price of the shells. I was allowed to go on the dove shoots to pick up birds. On Sunday afternoons Charles would take me with him to the clay pits for target practice at cans and old bottles. If I hit as many as he did he'd threaten not to bring me again.

Daddy would come down on weekends to visit. He hunted and fished with Charles on Saturdays. On Sunday mornings he would read the funny papers to me. His favorite comic strip was "Maggie and Jiggs." He thought they looked and acted like Uncle Ross and Auntie. He got a big kick out of substituting the names and reading it as "Auntie and Uncle Ross."

Alice Hammond, a colored woman, had cooked for Granny for years and she stayed on after Granny died. Alice made fresh hot rolls every day and I buttered and ate four at every meal. We still had a few chickens in the yard and Alice would chase one down in the yard, sling it by the neck till it was dead, then scald it and pick the feathers. I wouldn't have any part in helping her with the chickens but I would help her shell peas and butter beans. Sometimes I enjoyed ironing the handkerchiefs for her. I would lend a hand in most everything except making up the beds. As soon as she plumped up the big feather mattresses I would jump right in the middle of them and sink out of sight.

Alice had a daughter my age named Shirley. In the summertime Alice would bring Shirley to work with her so we could play together. Alice didn't get much help out of me on those days because Shirley and I played dolls and house and had tea parties. One day we were playing dentist and we glued a boy's teeth shut with peanut butter.

Growing up in a small town is an experience every American child should have. We had the freedom to go everywhere and the security of being looked after by everybody in town. The infinite variety of things we found to do we could never have done in a city. We walked the banks of the levee picking wild blackberries and plums. Sometimes we'd take a picnic lunch and go to the woods to pick lilies of the valley. The railroad track dead-ended in Elba and we often watched for the train and placed nails and pennies on the tracks so they were mashed flat. If we felt especially daring after the train left town, we walked the railroad track over the river. We'd ride our bicycles to the dam to go fishing or spend all day at the swimming pool until our lips turned blue from the cold artesian-well water. We always floated a watermelon in the pool and when we got too cold to swim we knew the watermelon was chilled enough to cut and eat. Occasionally the city would rope off the downtown at night so we could skate in the streets.

One day when I couldn't think of anything fun to do I decided to show one of my friends the new funeral home Uncle Ross had built for the insurance company. I didn't know who he thought would use it since everyone in Elba sat up all night with their dead at home, and all the funeral services were held at church. The only business I expected the place to do was the embalming. Uncle Ross had more faith than I did and he included a large parlor and a Hammond organ and two Cadillac hearses. I didn't believe Uncle Ross was going to revolutionize the burying business—in Elba—anytime soon.

Anyhow, I took my friend through the building and out the back where the hearses were parked. Cadillacs were not common in Elba, so we decided to examine them. One had a new casket in the back that had not yet been unloaded. We opened the door and climbed in the back of the hearse with the casket. "Look," I said, "there's a hidden button on the side that makes the top open." I pushed the button to show my friend the magic trick, but instead of finding the casket empty, there lay a corpse. We ran home as fast as we could, leaving the casket lid up, the hearse door open and our bicycles behind.

Elba was not only an exercise for stretching the imaginations of young minds, it was also a good grooming ground for young talent. Because there were so few young people in Elba someone was always needed to take part in some activity. And I was always ready, willing and able and had the energy to back it up.

The Elba School went from first through twelfth grades. The elementary school and high school were joined together with the gym and cafeteria. When the Elba High School band needed new members the band director recruited students from the elementary grades. You were only required to be big enough to tote a horn. I became a majorette in the fourth grade, and later on when we needed a B-flat tenor saxophone I learned to play one. I continued to take dancing lessons from a lady who came in once a week from another town, and when the recital was held I performed tap, ballet and toe.

Mother insisted I take elocution, so at assembly I would be called on to recite poems. I took part in the plays because I lived in town and could make the rehearsals. I sang in the choir at church and when there was no organist for the Sunday night services I learned to play the organ. When the local newspaper needed someone to write the school news column, I accepted the job.

My first love was the piano. Uncle Ross took me to Montgomery and let me pick out the one I wanted and bought it for me. About that time Poncy Brock moved to Elba to teach piano and I had the good fortune to be one of her students. She set up a practice schedule for me and planned my program of study several years ahead. I had always had the ambition; now

I had clearly defined goals and excellent instruction. Poncy inspired me and I worked hard. I found new rewards in practicing. I was so serious about my piano practice that I refused to be interrupted by my friends. For my ninth-grade recital I played "Rondo Capriccioso" by Mendelssohn. I felt a joy and satisfaction in my keyboard accomplishments and I had a burning ambition to be a concert pianist. That was the only serious thought I had about having a lifetime career. I was so earnest in fact that later when we planned to move from Elba I begged and pleaded with Mother to send me to a private school with a good music department so I could concentrate all my time on my piano studies. Mother was unconvinced that I would be happy in the strict confines of a boarding school.

Nothing very exciting ever happened in Elba. That was one of the nicest things about the town. Events were more or less predictable, which gives one a feeling of solidarity and stability. Life is easy and peaceful. People are relaxed and even talk slow.

Almost everybody in the town is related—either by blood or marriage. Everybody in town knows everybody else. Elba is not on a main highway, so very few outsiders ever came through town unless they had taken a wrong road and got lost. If a car came through Elba with an out-of-state tag everybody in town knew about it. There's an old saying, "Telephone, telegraph, tell-a-woman and the news will pass." That's the way it worked.

I remember one time a Cadillac automobile with a California license plate came through town and stopped at the flowing well on the square for some water. Well, the whole town was talking about that car. By the end of the week the driver was a movie star who looked like Clark Gable and was probably on his way to Florida. One time a car came through with a New York license plate and everybody said there was a gangster in it.

Weekdays were slow in Elba. Finding a store unattended on a weekday was not unusual. The proprietor might be visiting down the street or he might have gone home to do something for his wife. In the afternoons everybody gathered at the local drugstore for a fountain Coke or a milkshake.

Saturdays were busy days in Elba. The farmers would come in from the country to stock up for the week. The square would be crowded with pickup trucks and a few mules and wagons. The menfolks would sit on wooden benches in front of the stores and talk politics, crops and weather while the women-folks shopped for materials and patterns and groceries.

On Saturday mornings I met my friends at the picture show to watch the Westerns starring Gene Autry or Hopalong Cassidy and the weekly serials with Superman and the Lone Ranger. The boys got by with thumping spitballs but if they got caught with peashooters they were kicked out.

When I was twelve years old Uncle Ross let me drive all the way from Elba to Cullman—250 miles. When Auntie found out about it she was mad as a wet hen, but it was too late to undo it; I had learned to drive and I loved it. Most of the old-timers had learned to drive before people were licensed, so out of tradition they found it acceptable for young people to drive before they were sixteen years old.

Mother bought Charles and me a T-model Ford. It didn't use much gas but we had to stop every few miles and put a gallon of water in the radiator. Then Uncle Ross took me to a stock-car race in Dothan, and my fascination with cars was fixed.

Whoever had a car would go by and pick up the rest of our crowd until we were packed like sardines. One of the boys got a brand-new Chevrolet that had 90 miles per hour marked on the speedometer. We didn't believe the car would go that fast so we challenged him and ten of us piled in his car to witness the test. We went to the top of one of the highest hills on the highway and with the accelerator fully depressed we went from the top to the bottom of the hill. When we reached the bottom the needle of the speedometer bounced past 90 and around to 0.

One time I was riding around with a carload of girls and boys and we decided to go to the drive-in theater. After counting heads we discovered we didn't have enough money to pay everybody's way in, so two of the girls got in the trunk of the car. Sometimes we'd get two or three carloads of boys and girls and go park at the cemetery and tell ghost stories.

What I appreciate most about growing up in Elba is the Christian influence the people in the community had on my life. Sundays belonged to the Lord. I attended church all day on Sundays. I went to Sunday school and church in the morning, choir practice in the afternoon and Training Union and church Sunday night.

We had revivals in Elba once or twice a year. When I was about fourteen, I was attending a week-long revival at the First Baptist Church, where I was a member. The meetings seemed to be charged with the Holy Spirit. At one of the services the pastor gave the call for people to join the church or rededicate their lives. At that moment I felt a tremendous physical urge to present myself to the front of the church. That night I went forward and publicly rededicated my life to Christ.

I've never had an experience to equal that one before or since. It was just like some other force had taken over my body and was moving inside me. From then on God became very real to me. He seemed alive instead of some remote abstract being. I prayed every night as if God were in the room with me. He seemed so close I felt I could reach out and put my hand in his. His presence filled the room when I prayed and I knew he heard everything I said. I knew he was aware of my every thought, feeling and need. From then on I never felt I needed to go to people to talk about my problems and troubles. I talked everything over with God. I felt satisfied knowing he understood.

When you dedicate your life, you commit your life totally to God. When you say, "Lord, take my life and do with it what you will—it's not my life anymore, it's your life; use it to your glory," only then do you lose your life and only when you lose your life can you be born again and have a new life in Christ. I believe that formula will work for anyone. Say those words and see if the Holy Spirit fills your life. If you turn your life over to Christ you had better hold on—there's no telling where or how the Lord will use you.

My faith was not a thing that I shared with people. It was just between me and God. I tried to live my life so that people could see Christ working through me. My greatest frustrations in life are not being able to live up to God's expectations.

The most significant change in my life was that whenever I had to make a decision, I considered whether my choice would be acceptable in his sight. I'm not sure I've always made the right decision, but I know God knows that I've never taken any step without prayerful contemplation. And all my life I've prayed for wisdom to make the right choice.

Mother became restless living in Elba. She said she loved Elba and she wanted to be buried in Elba but she didn't want to be buried alive in Elba. So Mother and I moved to Washington, D.C., where she hoped life would be a little more exciting. Charles stayed in Elba with Auntie and Uncle Ross.

The period when Uncle Jimmy was governor I refer to as the "four fat years" and the period when he wasn't governor I call the "four lean years." It was during the four lean years that we lived in Washington.

Mother got a job working in the State Department for the Reciprocity Committee. We were forced to live on the small salary she made because none of Mother's family wanted her to go to Washington in the first place. In their opinion, the city was a den of iniquity and no place for a nice woman to live, let alone take a young girl.

Shortly after we arrived Mother was invited to a tea at the White House by Bess Truman, which was a direct result of my uncle's having supported Truman for president. Mother decided to take me along. We got all dressed up in our finest clothes. We didn't have enough money to take a cab, so we rode the bus. We laughed all the way to Pennsylvania Avenue about riding the bus to the White House but we didn't want anyone to laugh *at* us, so we rode one stop past the White House and walked back so no one would see us getting off the bus.

Before we got to the White House Mother stopped and said, "Would you please look at the seams in my hose and see if they are straight?"

I bent down and straightened the seams.

"Do I look all right?" Mother asked.

"Perfect," I answered.

We got into the receiving line, and just before Mother took Bess Truman's hand she looked down and said, "Oh, my Lord, Cornelia, I've got on mismatched shoes." She had on one shoe that was a low-cut pump and one that was a high-cut pump. They didn't match at all. So there she was, standing in line in the White House with one shoe of one pair and one of another pair and I had looked at her feet and had not even noticed the mistake. Mrs. Truman was very gracious and when she asked about Uncle Jimmy Mother stopped worrying about her mismatched shoes.

When we left the tea, Mother took me on the public tour of the White House. We went through the gallery of First Ladies' portraits, and there Mother pointed out a portrait of one of our relatives, Frances Folsom, who married Grover Cleveland when she was a nineteen-year-old girl. She looked like all the Folsoms I knew. She had coal-black hair, beautiful blue eyes and fair skin. Her portrait looked very much like the young pictures of my mother and my Uncle Jimmy. I was very proud.

In Washington I attended Alice Deal Junior High School, which was situated in a predominantly Jewish neighborhood. I had not been exposed to any religious customs except Protestant. I felt terribly left out because all my friends went to Hebrew classes on Saturday. On Jewish holidays we had so many absent students in our classroom the teacher couldn't give new lessons, so we were allowed to read.

We held a mock presidential election at the school in 1952 and I was the campaign manager for Adlai Stevenson. Most of the children were from Republican families and of course Eisenhower won.

After working in Washington for a year Mother and I moved back to Elba because Uncle Jimmy was making plans to run for governor again. He announced early in 1954 that he would seek a second term, and when his campaign got under way he came to Elba and made a speech on the town square in front of the courthouse.

Mother held a big barbecue after the speaking and invited all the people traveling with the campaign. Uncle Jimmy was shaking hands when I walked over to him. Before I could open my mouth he patted me on the head and said, "What's your name, honey?"

I said, "Uncle Jimmy, this is Cornelia. Don't you remember me?"

He said, "Why, of course, Cornelia, you've just grown so much I didn't recognize you."

174

George holding Uncle Jimmy's speech at the January 1955 Inaugural.

George Wallace was at the speaking and the barbecue too, since he was Uncle Jimmy's campaign manager for south Alabama. That was the second time I remember seeing George Wallace. If I had known then that I would one day become his wife I would have taken a closer look, but I wasn't interested in seeing anybody but Uncle Jimmy. He had been like a father to me and I had missed him sorely.

The campaign slogan was "Y'all come." The gimmick was the car caravan. The sound truck would pull into a town announcing that Big Jim Folsom would speak, and the cars would follow behind—covered with "Y'all come" bumper stickers and blowing horns. Everybody in the town would stop and stare.

The campaign was to end with a big rally in Montgomery the night before Election Day. The site of the rally was the Alabama Coliseum, which Uncle Jimmy had built during his first administration. It seated 10,000 and the place had never been filled since it was built. Nobody believed he was going to be able to pull this thing off. They expected the rally to flop and cause him to lose the election—at least that's what his opponents hoped.

Cars came from all four corners of the state, converging on Montgomery early in the day. There were cars lining the highways outside the Coliseum for miles. By 6 P.M. every seat in the place was filled.

It was the biggest political gathering that had ever assembled in the State of Alabama. That rally was probably the forerunner of big-time political rallies. Very few politicians, even today, can draw that kind of crowd.

The rally kickoff was at 7 P.M. The first thing on the program was the Elba High School band playing the national anthem. I was still a majorette, only I was in the ninth grade and I had matured into a young lady of fifteen years. I was so excited to be marching out with a peppy cadence, I was strutting until I thought my hips were going to pop out of their sockets. When the band got halfway into the Coliseum, they turned out all the lights and said, "Ladies and gentlemen, the Elba High School band and Governor Folsom's niece, Cornelia Ellis," and then put a spotlight on me. That was probably one of the biggest thrills I ever had in my whole life.

George Wallace introduced Uncle Jimmy. It was the first time I ever appeared in public on the same program with him. George gave a speech that really set the crowd on fire. As he says himself, "I brought that crowd to a fever pitch and brought on Jim Folsom." When Uncle Jimmy came on stage to make his speech, the crowd was out of control.

The next day the voters of Alabama went to the polls in the Democratic primary and nominated Uncle Jimmy governor for a second term by a landslide vote without a runoff, which was tantamount to election. It was the biggest vote any governor had ever received in Alabama. With my uncle's election as governor assured, Mother decided that she would like to return to Montgomery to live, so in the summer of 1954 we moved back to Montgomery.

Chapter 14

I ENTERED Sidney Lanier High School in September of 1954. The academic curriculum was equivalent to junior college. All through school I had managed to make A's and B's in every subject, despite the fact that I had made nine school changes in nine years, but the first semester at Lanier my grades dropped drastically. The second semester I pulled most of them up and by the time I reached my junior and senior years in high school I was achieving at my usual level.

Although I had to make an adjustment in my studies at Lanier, the education I received proved to be invaluable when I entered college. I was able to make good grades by spending a relatively small time studying.

My favorite class at Lanier was mechanical drawing. I chose it as my elective for two years. During the second year I drew a set of house plans complete with blueprints and elevations and then built a model house. From that class I was able to obtain a job with the Highway Department in the summer as an engineer's assistant. Two other summers I worked as a reading clerk for the Alabama Senate at the Capitol.

The same year I entered Lanier, Charles had enrolled as a freshman at the University of Alabama. He was majoring in Business Administration and took courses in insurance and planned to work with Uncle Ross in the insurance business. During his freshman year Charles married Betty Joyce Watson, his high-school sweetheart.

On the weekends Mother had taken a fancy to following the University of Alabama football team. She had encouraged one of my brother's friends from Elba, Jimmy Bowdoin, to accept a football scholarship at the university and felt obliged to attend the football games to offer moral support to Jimmy and to urge the team on to victory. As it turned out, there were very few victories. Even with Bart Starr quarterbacking, the team very seldom won a game. Paul "Bear" Bryant was coaching at Texas A & M, and the string of defeats Alabama suffered for several years influenced the university officials' decision to persuade Bear Bryant to come back to Tuscaloosa as head coach.

After every game we would wait outside the dressing-room door and Jimmy would come out with his head down and usually a few tears in his eyes.

I was a teen-ager in the mid-1950s, which made me a product of the rock 'n' roll craze. Ducktail haircuts and pegged pants were the vogue. The jitterbug was a thing of the past and the dance of the day was the bop. The Searchers, the Drifters and the Platters led the charts of hit rock 'n' roll records.

I continued to take piano lessons but I never found the teacher-pupil relationship I had had with Poncy Brock, although I did find it later with a voice teacher named Bill Williams only to have him die of a heart attack. I concentrated most of my energies on establishing new friends at Lanier, and as my practice time at the piano diminished, my prospects for a career as a concert pianist slowly dwindled.

One summer when I was a clerk for the Alabama State Senate, Lily Mae Caldwell of the *Birmingham News* came to Montgomery with the then reigning Miss Alabama to introduce her to the two houses of the Legislature. Lily Mae was in charge of the Miss Alabama contest, and when Mother introduced me to her she said, "Ruby, you have a very pretty daughter. Why don't you enter her in the Miss Alabama contest?"

"She's not old enough," Mother answered.

Lily Mae explained that the girls enter two or three years before they are old enough to be considered for the title of Miss Alabama. So the next year I prepared to enter the Miss Alabama contest as Miss Lily Mae had suggested, although I was

179

only seventeen at the time and not eligible to compete for the title. I played "Clair de Lune" by Debussy on the piano and was presented with a certificate as one of the top ten out of seventy-five girls under the age of eighteen who competed that year. It was more a talent contest than a beauty contest. Some years later this contest was moved to Mobile and became the Junior Miss America Pageant.

The next year I entered the Miss Alabama contest again. I performed in the talent competitions a popular rendition of "Around the World," playing the piano and singing as I accompanied myself. We had several days of competition, and I was now eligible for the title. I was severely disappointed when I was eliminated the first time around, since I had expected to move up and improve my position. When I was dropped so early in the competition, I decided never again to enter the Miss Alabama contest.

Auntie had gone to Birmingham to chaperone me for the contest and had witnessed all the competitions and my participation, and when she learned that I had been dropped from the list of eligibles she turned around and in a huff said, "Well, all the judges must be tone-deaf and half blind."

We didn't even bother to stick around to see who placed in the finals, but departed early in the day for Montgomery. Auntie spent the night with Mother and me before leaving for Elba early the next morning. The three of us had breakfast together and when I left for school Mother and Auntie were still at the table talking about Uncle Ross's upcoming court case of alleged income tax evasion.

At 1:30 P.M. I was in glee club when a voice on the speaker system instructed the teacher to send me to the Dean of Girls' office. I didn't think I had violated any school rules but she wasn't known for handing out rewards either. My apprehension grew as I approached her office but the minute I walked through the door I knew that my second-guessing was not right. Rachel's Aunt Mary Olive Carnley was there with that look on her face of something terribly wrong.

I knew before she said a word that something had happened to somebody in the family. It was hard for her to get the facts out because she was searching for a gentle way to tell me, but when she finally got all the words together it was: Uncle Ross has committed suicide.

The humiliation of an income tax evasion charge brought against him, which was politically motivated, was too much for Uncle Ross. He faced losing his fortune and his business but he couldn't face losing his good name.

Auntie went against Uncle Ross's wishes and held his funeral in the First Baptist Church instead of the funeral parlor he had built. Auntie had always wanted Uncle Ross to join the church and she wasn't about to give up her fight just because he was dead.

When we lost Uncle Ross we lost the financial and emotional mainstay of our family. He had always looked after all of the Folsoms and his own relatives as if we were all the children he never had. I missed him terribly but it was Charles who suffered the most in every way. He had lost his surrogate father but he had also lost his future career in the family insurance business. Uncle Ross had been the guiding light in his life and now the light had gone out.

In 1956 the National Democratic Convention was being held in Chicago. Uncle Jimmy was not able to attend the convention, so he sent Jamelle and Mother to represent him. Rachel and Melissa and I were allowed to go along. We took the train from Montgomery to Chicago and stayed at the same hotel where all the candidates had hospitality suites. Each governor had a reserved box at the convention hall, and every night we would go to the hall and watch the activities that were taking place on the floor.

George Wallace was a member of the Alabama delegation and led the platform committee. John Kennedy was trying to win the vice-presidential nomination and all the Kennedys were working toward that end. George Wallace introduced Eunice Kennedy to the Alabama delegation when they were in caucus because the Alabama delegates favored the Kennedy nomination for vice-president.

It was an exciting convention. Governor Frank Clement from Tennessee made the keynote address. He was young, handsome and dynamic. He dramatically finished his speech by

181

saying, "Lord, take my hand and lead me on." John Kennedy also addressed the convention. He was equally handsome and dynamic. I thought the Democratic Party was unusually fortunate to have two such bright and articulate young men as Kennedy and Clement. I was full with hope that the Democratic Party had a great future, and I was certain John Kennedy would eventually become President of the United States. Adlai Stevenson won the Democratic nomination that year and Estes Kefauver was selected as the vice-presidential nominee.

In the years between 1955 and 1959, while Uncle Jimmy was serving his second term as governor, Martin Luther King came to Montgomery, Alabama, to stage his first bus boycott. There were some sit-in demonstrations down at the dime store, where the lunch counters had been segregated for years, as was every other public facility in the South. There were separate restrooms for blacks and whites, separate sitting areas on the buses, separate seating places in the theaters, separate water fountains. It was a way of life in the South. We had grown up with those customs and we felt comfortable with them. Once the changes began to be forced, the relations between blacks and whites became strained and uneasy.

After the bus boycott there was Autherine Lucy. She was the first black woman ever to enroll as a student at the University of Alabama. Uncle Jimmy was chairman of the Board of Trustees of the university, a position held traditionally by all the governors of Alabama, and when Autherine Lucy came to the campus to try to enroll, Uncle Jimmy met with the board behind closed doors to decide how to handle her enrollment. This could have been the first stand in the schoolhouse door. "There's no black person who wants to stay in school with white people for very long," Uncle Jimmy said. He advised the board to "Let her enroll at the university. She probably won't stay a week." Frankly, no white person in Alabama believed that her intentions for wanting to enter the university were sincere. There was no doubt that the effort to get Autherine Lucy in the university was sponsored by an out-of-state group that was trying to see if they could achieve integration in the South, and the white people resented the interference with their traditions.

All these things together tended to cast my uncle in the role of a liberal. People said Jim Folsom was too soft on the question of integration.

In the spring of 1957, during my senior year at Lanier, Rachel and I enrolled for the fall semester at the University of Alabama. I had spent many weekends at the university, visiting and staying overnight in almost every sorority house. I had many friends on campus but in the spring, when the sororities were staging the rush parties in Montgomery, Rachel and I were noticeably left out when the invitations were issued. I began to suspicion that something had gone wrong, that it was more than an oversight. Finally, one of my friends who belonged to a sorority advised me that if Rachel and I went to the university and went out for rush, we would probably not receive an invitation to join any sorority on campus. I was shocked and terribly crushed to hear this news because I had always wanted to attend the University of Alabama and I had never even thought about going to any other college.

I knew the University of Alabama was the kind of campus that, to enjoy, you almost had to belong to a sorority. I felt I had already experienced so much hurt and loss that I really did not want to subject myself to the cruelty of a situation where I would be ostracized from the social life of the university.

I told Rachel what I expected to happen and I advised her not to enroll at the University of Alabama. Rachel did not take my advice seriously. She went on up to the university, went out for rush and was dropped one by one from every sorority list. Rachel was severely hurt by this rejection and in fact, to my way of thinking, she never got over it.

Instead of going to the university, I enrolled as a day student at Huntingdon College in Montgomery, where there was a good music department, and lived at home with Mother.

On September 25, 1957, something happened to me that changed the course of my life. That day I had driven Mother up to the Capitol because she wanted to talk to Uncle Jimmy about a personal matter. I decided not to go into the Capitol with her, so I remained outside. I sat in my Chevrolet convertible under the shade of a big oak tree listening to some music on the radio. As I was sitting there a cowboy rode in front of me on horseback. I was a little astonished by this because normally you do not see horses on the Capitol grounds. Then the disc jockey said, "Today in Montgomery we are celebrating Hank Williams Memorial Day." All of a sudden I realized the horse was part of a parade.

Mother came out of the Capitol and I suggested that we stay and watch the parade. We went down and parked on Dexter Avenue behind some cars that were lining up to carry some country music singers who had come in to honor the South's most famous troubadour. As the parade was about to get started it became evident that someone had miscounted and that they were short one convertible for the parade.

One of the men in charge of the parade walked over and asked if I'd mind if they used my car. I said, "Of course not." In a few minutes he walked back with Don and Phil Everly, who had recorded the hit record "Bye Bye Love." They were very apologetic about pirating my automobile.

Mother got out of the car and I started to get out too, when Phil turned and said, "We would like to have you ride in the parade with us." So I did. Phil and Don sat on the back and I rode in the front with the driver.

At the end of the parade Phil turned to me and said, "Do you plan to come to the performance tonight? We are going to sing and I'd like it very much if you would come and hear us." I told him I would. Since Rachel was at the university with most of my other friends, I called Melissa, who was still in high school, and a friend of mine named Jean Holland, and at seven o'clock we went to the Montgomery City Auditorium where the songfest was to take place, the same place where they had held the funeral for Hank Williams.

All the stars performed. Phil and Don sang "Bye Bye Love." After Phil finished the song, he sent his managers, Wesley and Lester Rose, sons of the late Fred Rose, of the Acuff-Rose Publishing Company, into the auditorium to take me backstage. Phil asked if I would like to do something after the show, and since he didn't have a car, I told him that we would wait and take him along.

When the performance was over, Phil, Don, Melissa, Jean and I went to the Governor's Mansion and had some refreshments. Melissa was giving a tour of the house and as we passed through the kitchen she said, "This is the kitchen, this is the stove, this is the refrigerator and here's the dishwasher."

To that, Phil chimed in "We have a dishwasher at home, too: Don's wife, Sue." Realizing that Don had a wife, I decided that the company of a young married boy was no place for Melissa and Jean to be, so we left Melissa and Jean at the house and took Don back to the hotel.

Phil and I went to an all-night café. He put several quarters in the jukebox and punched all the country music records and we sat down and had a long deep talk about Phil's childhood and growing up and the years of hardship his family had had before their success.

Phil had to leave early the next morning because they had another engagement so we stayed out later than I normally would have. We ended up back at my house and I played some classical piano music for him. Then we sat on the couch and talked. I suddenly realized that there was something about this boy that I liked very much. He was warm and sincere and earnest; he had a quality—a genuineness—about him that I had not seen in many boys his age. It seemed that for his years he had experienced enough of life to have a sense of values that I appreciated.

When Phil and I parted company that night, we parted with a promise to write each other. For the next several months he called me from almost every town in the country, usually at one or two o'clock at night, after he had finished performing his shows. We wrote to each other; then when he saw that he might have a break at Christmas, he decided to come to Alabama and visit so we could get to know each other better. He came and spent a few days in Montgomery and we talked to his mother by long-distance telephone and he asked me if I would like to meet his family. I took him to the Highway Department building, where we went down to the coffee shop for a Coke with my daddy. My feelings for Phil grew stronger in that visit. There was so much about him I liked and admired. He was warm, sensitive and tender and, unlike any other boy I had ever known, he was a very deep thinker.

It was impossible for a day to go by without my thinking of Phil, because every time I got in my car and turned on the radio, one of his songs would be playing. He had a new record called "Wake Up, Little Susie" that was number one on all the charts and sold a million records.

Phil and Don were scheduled to appear at the Paramount Theatre during the Christmas holidays. Knowing that I had Christmas vacation from Huntingdon College at the same time, Phil invited me to come up to New York to spend the Christmas holidays with him.

I talked over the proposal with Mother and told her that I had some doubts about whether it was the right thing to do. I felt somehow that being with Phil while he was on a working tour would not enhance our relationship and that by going to New York I would put myself in a position of going after him rather than him coming to see me. It was not a situation that I felt I would be very comfortable in. Mother was delighted, not that Phil had invited me to New York but that she had an opportunity to use me as an excuse to make the trip herself. So, from the time I told Mother, nothing would do her except that we go to New York City. I told Phil that Mother and I would be there.

Mother and I arrived a day ahead of Phil. There's not a city in the world that Mother has ever been where she didn't know somebody or feel comfortable. If she didn't know someone before she went, she knew somebody as soon as she arrived. She made friends out of strangers.

By the time Phil had arrived, I already had my social schedule lined up. I had agreed to go to an ice hockey game with a friend of my mother's that night. When Phil arrived, I told him of my plans and invited him to come along. He was obviously hurt by the fact that I had not waited on him before planning my evening. The trip in itself proved to be more disastrous to our relationship than I had ever imagined it could be. Phil had social obligations of his own with Archie Beyer, president of Cadence Record Company, who also had a young, attractive daughter, Jackie. I saw Phil briefly during the holidays but our commitments to other people and other places, along with his schedule of four shows at the Paramount Theatre, left very little time for us to be together. Phil spent New Year's Eve in the company of the president of his record company, the presi-

186

dent's daughter, and his managers and I spent New Year's Eve with Mother and Paul Anka.

While I was busy with my social life and a faltering romance, Mother had been busy making contacts and meeting new people. Somehow or another, she had managed to acquire a new friend: Mr. Leo Cohen at the MGM studios. One day while we were in New York she came to me and invited me to go to the MGM studios to meet her new friend. While we were sitting in Mr. Cohen's office he looked at me point blank and said, "Young lady, how would you like to have a screen test?" I asked him if I could think it over and told him that since I was a musician and not an actress, I would prefer to have a chance to audition for the MGM record label.

When I told him I was not interested in accepting his offer of a screen test, I thought Mother would jump out the window of that building. I know it must have been a terrific disappointment to her. Perhaps it was an opportunity that I should have taken but at the time I did not feel that I was qualified, and I had no interest in speaking lines that I considered dry, and particularly the idea of being a young actress in Hollywood, waiting for parts, did not appeal to me.

Mr. Cohen said that they would be glad to give me a record audition. I agreed to come back in the summer and audition and make a record with the MGM company. I left New York City without resolving any of the differences between Phil and me. My relationship with Phil was left in limbo.

I should have been excited, as any young girl would be, by the offer of a screen test from MGM. On the trip home, all that was in my mind was the thought that I wished I had not made the trip and that I had continued to meet Phil in Montgomery, where we had such a beautiful friendship. I wondered if I would ever see Phil again.

The offer to make a record with MGM gave me an opportunity to take all the music training I had had in my life and do something with it. I was well aware that I would not be able to have a classical music career, and I saw this as an opportunity to take my talents and all my experience and put it into one package. Rock 'n' roll music was big in those days and country music was becoming big. All the star singers wrote their

Recording for MGM.

own songs, and recorded them, and most of them played guitars. I purchased a $19 guitar and a chart and spent many hours alone teaching myself to play.

Buying a cheap guitar was a mistake. I thought it was better not to spend a lot of money, not knowing whether I would learn to play, but it's a deterrent for anyone ambitious to play the guitar because the strings cut into your fingers until they are bruised and bleeding. I did have some misgivings about continuing with my guitar playing because I was afraid that the calluses on my fingers would hurt my touch on the piano. However, there was something about the guitar that I liked more than the piano. You could hold the instrument close to you and get the feel of it. After experimenting with the guitar for a while, I realized that I probably would have loved the violin because there is something about being able to hold an instrument close to you and caress it while you play.

As summer grew near, the time was nearing for me to make my return trip to New York and cut the record with MGM. I began to look around for something that I thought was a salable act. I knew that making a record in itself would not necessarily mean success. There were no girls playing guitars, and I envisioned a group of three girls all dressed in pastel-colored skirts, pink, yellow and blue, with guitars covered in a matching color, singing a trio. This was my idea of a unique act and one that I thought would be very successful on the stage and with the public.

I enlisted two of my friends at Huntingdon College, and one of the girls never learned to play the guitar so I ended up with Nancy Baughcum and myself.

Nancy was from Atlanta, Georgia. I had first seen her when she pantomimed a Spike Jones record in a talent contest on campus. She was a great comedienne. Nancy and I began to spend a lot of time after our classes playing the guitar and singing and appearing at the local theaters for the Saturday-morning stage shows. We appeared at Montgomery and Selma and even went as far as Columbus, Georgia, to sing and play our guitars.

In 1958 there was another governor's race. Uncle Jimmy could not succeed himself and was therefore not a candidate, and George Wallace announced his candidacy. Mother jumped on his bandwagon without hesitating. She said because George had been my uncle's campaign manager, we were obligated to support him. The slogan for the campaign was "Win with Wallace" and the first rally scheduled early in the year in Ozark. Nancy Baughcum and I had been rehearsing our act and looking for an opportunity to perform and sing in public. I thought a good way to gain a little experience and also help George Wallace would be to sing and travel with his campaign. The number-one hit record for that year was "Sugartime" by the Chordettes. It was a catchy tune and hard to beat. I decided to write a campaign song, changing the lyrics but using the melody. I wrote a song for George Wallace's campaign that went:

> Wallace in the morning, Wallace in the evening,
> Wallace at suppertime.
> When you cast your ballot,
> Well, that is Wallace time.

On the opening day of the campaign Mother took us to the home of Foy Halstead, a Folsom friend and Wallace supporter where some of the Montgomery people were gathering to travel to Ozark. George's brother was there, and Nancy and I sang the song I had composed to him. He liked it and told us to go on to Ozark. When we arrived in Ozark some of the head people in the Wallace campaign met to decide whether Nancy and I should perform. Minnie Pearl was traveling with the campaign at the time, and Lamar Morris was playing lead guitar with the band. I sat in a restaurant and talked with Lamar. Lamar had played the guitar on several recording sessions that I had taped at WBAM Radio in Montgomery. He and I had become big friends and I was always encouraging Lamar to take his talents to Nashville, telling him he was the best guitarist in these parts. (He eventually did and ultimately married Lucretia Williams, the daughter of Audrey and the late Hank Williams.)

While we were waiting to find out whether we would be allowed to sing, Lamar said that shortly he would be campaigning with the candidate who was going to be the next Governor of Alabama.

I said, "But Lamar, you are already."

He smiled and said, "I'm talking about somebody else," but he refused to tell me who he meant. I thought it was a big joke because George was favored to win and everybody was confident that he would be elected. Later Lamar began playing for John Patterson, who ultimately defeated George Wallace and won the governorship.

As Nancy and I stood by the platform waiting for our turn to go on stage, someone came up to us and said we would not be allowed to sing because we did not have union cards. Although the Musicians' Union does not require one to have a union card to sing, a card is required to play instruments.

Nancy and I had brought our guitars and planned to accompany ourselves when we sang. Of course, I was extremely disappointed that I was rebuked that day in Ozark. Right before George went on stage he stopped and told Nancy and me that he regretted that we would not be able to sing with him. On the way back to Montgomery I was bemoaning the fact that we had lost our opportunity to gain some valuable experience on-stage. Mother consoled me by saying that she was sure the reason we were not allowed to sing was because of my family ties—because I was a Folsom. The next day the *Montgomery Advertiser* ran a story which said I was rebuffed because I was Folsom kin. Once again my uncle's liberal stand on the segregation-integration question had prevented me from participating in something that I wanted very much to be a part of.

We named ourselves Sugar and Honey, and when the time came to go on our trip to New York, we realized that what we needed to be successful was a song that we had composed ourselves. We started working on the numbers and finished one called "It's No Summer Love." I did all the music and some of the lyrics and Nancy helped with completing the lyrics of the song. On the way to New York we had still not written the reverse side of the record. Mother drove and Nancy and I played our guitars, and before we arrived in New York City we had polished off the last bars of "Baby with the Barefoot Feet." When we finished the song, we decided without a doubt that "Baby with the Barefoot Feet" would be the hit side of our new record.

In those days all the girls were wearing full gathered skirts

191

and crinoline petticoats. The more petticoats you wore, the farther your dress would stand out. It was not uncommon for a girl to wear as many as six crinoline petticoats, all starched and ironed so that they were stiff as boards. The bad thing about this fashion was that when you traveled there was no way to pack your petticoats. When Nancy and I started to New York, we stuffed all our petticoats in brown paper bags. When we arrived in New York City to check into the Astor Hotel, we arrived in a station wagon that was about to be repossessed with six brown paper bags full of crinoline petticoats and two $19 guitars without cases. We dumped everything on the sidewalk, and everybody coming and going stopped and stared. I suppose they thought we were a band of gypsies, but that wasn't so bad because Mother had always wanted to be a gypsy. Now she had her own troupe of gypsies and, of all the cities of the world, in New York City.

The people at the music department of MGM wrote some arrangements for the songs that we had written. They were excited about "Baby with the Barefoot Feet." MGM had just sold over 3 million copies of the hit record "Purple People Eater," and they felt that this would be another hit for them. Leroy Holmes did our arrangements, Marty Craft was the A and R man for our session and "Sam the Man" Taylor played the saxophone. When we went into the studios, Connie Francis was just finishing her session of "Stupid Cupid," and we used her combo to record our songs.

I was overcome with anxiety during the session. Nancy and I did not sing our best because we never felt that the arrangements were right for our songs. I knew all the time we were singing that we needed to be in Nashville and have a Nashville sound behind us. I never thought that our record could become a hit.

Chapter 15

THE RECORD was a flop. The recording session behind us, Nancy —who was suffering homesick-itis—decided she wanted no part of the world of entertainment. We split up the team and she went home to her family in Georgia, which suited Mother fine because she envisaged her daughter as a solo act. I knew the split was inevitable. Even successful duo acts sooner or later come to a parting of the ways.

Mother called her cousin Peter Flournoy, who was the producer of a summer stock playhouse in Binghamton, New York, and he agreed to take me as an apprentice for the rest of the summer. Mother put me on a Greyhound bus in New York City. Both of us managed to hold back our tears until we were out of each other's sight—not an easy task as it was the first time we had ever been separated.

I worked as an apprentice to the janitor, I guess, because the only job I had all summer was sweeping the stage. We were supposed to have walk-ons and small parts plus acting workshops. We had no workshops and I had no parts. "What I learned was what I observed" from the many stars who came there with touring troupes. There was Victor Jory, Sir Cedric Hardwicke, Claude Dauphine, Hermione Gingold, Dennis Morgan, Wendy Barrie and Tallulah Bankhead. Tallulah was from Alabama and showing her age, so her contract called for pink footlights which she insisted made her look more youthful. Her days were spent secluded in her hotel room with her demanding habit. Wendy Barrie, recovering from the disillusionment of being dropped from the Revlon television commercials due to Mr. Revson's fancy for a younger face, offered me an unsolicited but sound bit of advice. "There's no place in this business for a nice girl like you. Go home and find a nice young man and get married."

Victor Jory's son and I became fast friends and corresponded for a while. Dennis Morgan was as charming offstage as on and graciously consented to pose for a picture with me for my hometown paper. The interviewer asked me if I planned to follow in Tallulah Bankhead's footsteps and I said no. I didn't have the courage to tell him that Jesus' was the only example I wanted to follow.

At the end of the summer, Rachel and I enrolled in Rollins College in Winter Park, Florida. During the first weeks, I went out for rush. In the course of the flurry of rush parties a boy who was dating a Chi Omega girl told me the girls were upset because they wanted very much to pledge me. The problem they ran into was a "No" recommendation on me from Montgomery. He said the girls had written and asked for a reason. The answer was that my uncle, Governor Folsom, was too liberal on the integration question. The girls felt that this was unfair—after all, some the northern sororities were already accepting black pledges—and they appealed to the National Board but were not able to override the vote of the alumni in Montgomery.

Meanwhile Melissa was making her own unsuccessful attempt to escape the prejudice by attending the University of Arkansas. The Kappa Kappa Gammas on campus there were so infuriated over the "No" recommendation she got that they allowed Melissa to live in the sorority house even though they were blocked from offering her a bid.

I decided not to try to outrun the race issue. If I went to another college in a different state, the recommendation would still come from Montgomery and it wouldn't change unless the alumni dropped dead. The thing that irked me most was that no one had bothered to ask me if I shared my uncle's views. The truth of the matter was they didn't bother to take note of the fact that I made a public speech through a YMCA program to a men's civic group in the Whitley Hotel in downtown Montgomery opposing integration. I chose the subject, wrote the speech and toned it down during the delivery only because the waiters were still clearing the tables.

Uncle Jimmy finally made the political mistake of his life— he reportedly received a Negro socially in the Governor's Mansion. The newspaper account went as follows: "Governor Folsom entertained New York Congressman Adam Clayton Powell at the Governor's Mansion where the two men had a drink of Scotch."

Uncle Jimmy, who drank bourbon, said, "That's a lie. I never had a drink of Scotch in my life."

Narrow-minded people called him a Negro lover. People with vision said he was a man twenty years ahead of his time. Whatever he was I was his only blood niece. I loved him like a father and I, along with his daughters, was feeling the repercussions of his unpopular stance.

My uncle had not publicly or privately advocated integrating the public school system. If he had opposed it he wouldn't have gotten any farther than the schoolhouse door. But injustice is as painful to a white governor's niece as it is to a black sharecropper's son. The fact remains—the schools were segregated under Governor Folsom and integrated under Governor Wallace. How ironic.

There were several reasons I went to Rollins College, the foremost being that Rollins had a well-established music department. My voice teacher commented on my report card that I did not seriously evaluate my own remarkable talent. I had clear, well-placed tones that ranged from contralto to lyric soprano. Yet when I went to audition for the Rollins chapel choir, although there were only six voice majors in my class, the choir director placed me in the tenor section, which meant he, too, improperly evaluated my voice and he also forgot the importance of choral training to a voice major.

The second reason I chose Rollins College was because it was one of the few schools in the nation, other than Florida Southern in Lakeland, that offered waterskiing for credit as part of the physical education program. I elected to take waterskiing as my physical education program. The skiing instructor was most encouraging to me because he said I was the most aggressive student he had. He began coaching me for the Rollins water-ski team, spending many hours training me to run the slalom course for competition. His name was Gramps and at fifty years of age, with one arm nubbed by a boat propeller, he was still able to do a complete 360-degree turn around on one trick ski.

For the time I was at Rollins I dated José Ochoa, who was a boy of Spanish descent. His family lived in Mexico City. José had returned to college after a tour on the world tennis circuit. He had been ranked as fifth in the world at one time and had close friendships with Rafael Trujillo, Jr., Pancho Gonzales, and many of the jet set. The social life that José had led while he was on the tennis circuit had broken his training and caused his ranking to drop drastically, so he and his family decided that it was time for him to put down his racket and pick up the books. He returned to Rollins and enrolled in the business administration school there.

José's Spanish friends thought I looked as Latin as they did and readily accepted me as one of their own, but I had a thing or two to learn about Latin customs. One afternoon while José and I were having a Coke at the local hangout, a boy I knew came over and innocently asked me to dance. José dramatically smashed his glass on the floor, grabbed the boy by the collar and invited him to go outside. I thought José had gone mad. In the true Latin tradition José viewed the overture as an insult because the boy had not asked his permission first.

I made a trip to Nashville to the disc jockey convention while I was in Rollins College and met Minnie Pearl, Hank Thompson, Eddy Arnold and many of the other country music stars. Mother introduced me to Jimmy Davis, who was Governor of Louisiana in addition to being a singer and a songwriter. Wherever a group gathered for fun and frolic, if Mother chanced to be in their midst she would lead them in "You Are My Sunshine." I told Governor Davis that he need never worry about the popularity of his song because, as I put it, "As long as Mother is alive, your song will never die."

I knew that if my career as a folksinger was going anywhere I had to find the proverbial "man with the cigar who would make me a star." I needed a manager. I needed the seasoning and polish a performer only gets from singing on-stage every night for months on end. I asked around Nashville for the name of the best personal manager in the business. The answer was always the same: "Tom Parker—but he's tied up with Elvis Presley—or Oscar Davis. Oscar might be available because he just dropped Jerry Lee Lewis." Under Oscar's supervision the blond head-shaking piano player demanded and got $300,000 for a motion-picture title song. Then on a tour in Europe Jerry Lee married a thirteen-year-old girl. Scandalous stories hit the newspapers back home so Oscar dropped him like a hot potato and Jerry Lee's career plummeted to the ground.

Nobody believed Oscar Davis would sign me because I was too green and he was too broke. Hank's widow, Audrey Williams, arranged an audition meeting in her home. Oscar liked me. He said I was different; I had class; I could write. He was confident he could sell me. Why not? He could sell oil to the Arabs.

This was the plan: Oscar would book me on stage shows for a year. I would write a hundred songs. The goal: a much-publicized concert in Carnegie Hall in New York City featuring me, my songs, my guitar and one spotlight.

I liked the idea. There was one hitch—finances. Mother overreacted and said she'd get the money, so eager was she to see me become a star. She had made Daddy a success; she had made Uncle Jimmy a success; now she was going to make me a success—as if by the measure of the successes of the people she loved she somehow proved her own ability and worth. Probably Mother could have been the biggest star of all if she had just had the encouragement. Anyway, over my protest, Mother wrote Oscar a check for $1,000 to seal the deal.

I returned to Rollins only to leave for good in February, when Oscar Davis booked me with Roy Acuff, who was about to make a trip overseas and needed a girl singer for his troop. Roy teamed me up with a girl named Melba Montgomery, who was from Florence, Alabama. Everyone in her family could sing and play an instrument. Melba got to Nashville by winning a singing contest but she preferred singing duets.

On our tour we had Roy Acuff headlining with his sidekick, Oswald, on banjo, steel guitarist Shot Jackson, fiddle player

Howdy Howard, Lonnie on bass fiddle, piano player Gene Webb, the Wilburn Brothers, and Melba and Connie, as Roy liked to call us. Melba and I played twin Martin guitars and wore square-dance-type dresses which we had had made in the United States before we left.

Melba and I practiced for a few weeks before departing, and for the first time I realized how terrible Nancy and I had sounded. Melba taught me everything I know about singing harmony, as well as the words to country songs I'd never heard. We sang one of Jean Shepard's songs called "I'll Take the Blame," and an old Eddy Arnold song called "Have I Told You Lately That I Love You?"

The first stop we made was at the Louisiana Hay Ride in Shreveport, Louisiana. Prior to our appearance in Shreveport, Roy discovered that Melba and I were not members of the Musicians' Union so he made arrangements for us to obtain a union card before we went onstage.

When Melba and I finished our songs we brought the house down. They roared, hollered and clapped for an encore. So Melba and I did, of all things, a chorus of "Bye Bye Love." I was excited and pulled on Melba's arm and said, "Melba, did you hear all that applause we got?" She said not to mention it, that all the other stars would be jealous. I hid my thrill at the moment in order not to offend our other country music friends. That was the first professional stage appearance I ever made. Roy was paying me $75 per week.

From Shreveport we went to Corpus Christi and San Antonio, Texas. We made our way to California, and from there we flew to Hawaii, where we stayed eight days, appearing at the Schofield Barracks at Hickman Air Force Base. We played at the hospital for soldiers who had been wounded in the Korean conflict.

Hawaii was like paradise. I thought surely I must have died and passed on to heaven. The sun shone every day and there was just enough breeze from the ocean to keep the air from ever becoming stale or heavy. We were given a special tour out to the sunken battleship *Arizona*, where many American soldiers were entombed at the bombing of Pearl Harbor. I felt very heavyhearted, knowing those boys below had given their lives for the few of us who were standing above, yet proud that we were all still enjoying the freedom they died to preserve.

We stayed at the Waikiki Hotel, where every evening someone would turn back the covers on our beds and place a small Vanda orchid on the pillow. The natives would stroll around at night playing their ukeleles and serenading us with native Hawaiian songs. The Hawaiians were fascinated with Roy Acuff and his troupe because they, too, play stringed instruments but they had never seen the likes of Shot Jackson's steel guitar. Roy Acuff, whom I learned to admire, love and respect, was one of the kindest people I think I ever met. He would do everything in his power to be fair and to keep everybody in his troupe happy. By Roy's own admission he is not a singer, but he made a heap of money letting other folks think he was. He is by unanimous agreement a master showman. The natives were thrilled and in return played some Hawaiian music for us. They taught us some Hawaiian songs and hulas and told us about the customs of their islands.

Melba and I continued to draw the loudest applause at every appearance. Although we were pleased we were somewhat embarrassed as we were considered the lowest act on the totem pole as far as public recognition goes. However, Roy was pleased that our act put the punch he needed in his show.

From Hawaii we flew to Australia, landing in Sydney. We did a show at the Old Sydney Auditorium, which proved to be a mistake for Roy. Roy had financed the tour out of his own pocket. Other American acts going to Australia at the time were drawing big crowds and taking in a lot of money at the door. But Australians, like the British, did not understand the American hillbilly folk humor. While music is easily translated from one country to another, it is very difficult for one country to interpret the humor of another country, even if the language is the same. It was the worst show we had during the tour. Roy realized his jokes were not going over with the crowd, and we finished up the show by doing more musical numbers than comedy routines.

One reason why Roy Acuff's humor was so difficult for the Australians to understand is because when we would say "Out in the country," they would say "Out back." Instead of a "ranch" they would say "station." They called the West "the bush country." For American humor to be understood in Australia almost every key word in the jokes would have had to be changed to a word that was used in Australia.

We made one other attempt at a stage show in Australia in Adelaide. That show was no more successful than the one in Sydney. We returned to Sydney and we were staying in a hotel. The first person that we ran into was the wrestler "Gorgeous George." Roy had known him before. In order to salvage something financially from the trip, Roy Acuff contracted with a local television station to film the first television series that was ever made in Australia. The television company would take the Australian rights and Roy would take the American rights. We moved into a boardinghouse and for the next two months we went to the television station every day to either film or rehearse the shows. Many days we would film as many as four shows.

We ended up doing 125 television shows for the series, which was called "Roy Acuff Open House." Roy eventually sold that series to individual stations and they were played in the areas of Bethesda, Maryland, Virginia, West Virginia and parts of Tennessee. The U.S. Government bought some of them to play for the troops overseas.

One day while we were at the boardinghouse Johnny Cash came by to pay a call. He sat on the couch and played a song that he was writing but had not finished called "How High Is the Water, Papa," which ended up as "Five Feet High & Rising."

One day in Australia when I was putting on my makeup to film one of the television shows, a telegraph messenger came in with a cablegram for me. When I opened it, it read, WE WERE MARRIED ON APRIL 13, 1959. MOTHER AND DR. AUSTIN. Before I had left Montgomery, Dr. Burton Forsythe Austin had become widowed. Mother and I had seen him on a couple of occasions and he seemed so lonely and asked Mother to call him while I was away. The last thing I said to Mother before I left was "to be sure and remember to call Dr. Austin. I know he is lonely and he would enjoy your company." I cried when I read the message but my tears were from joy. I had

200

worried about Mother so much. She had devoted her life to bringing me up and I hated to leave her alone. She had invested so much time and energy and love in me I realized she would feel a void when I left home. I was glad she had someone to love who would love her in return.

When we completed the filming of the television series Roy was asked to go to Japan and Korea to entertain the troops. Roy dedicated much of his time and energy to doing USO shows. I had hoped very much that he would go ahead and extend the tour to take in these countries, but most of the men who traveled with us were married and had families and Roy, being so conscientious of the needs of the people who worked for him, felt that they should be permitted to return home to their families before he took them on another tour.

After two and one half months of traveling we returned to the United States and landed at the Los Angeles International Airport. The weather was bad, which forced us to go to a motel and wait for approximately twenty-four hours before we could depart.

I immediately called Mother to tell her that I was back in the United States and she told me that Phil was in Los Angeles, where he would be doing the Roy Rogers–Dale Evans show. I decided to call Phil while I was passing through. When I rang the studio someone answered the phone and called Phil from rehearsal. We had a brief chat and he invited me to stay over for a few days and visit him in California. I declined the invitation because I did not feel it would be proper for me to stay without a chaperone.

Mother and Dr. Austin were waiting when our plane landed in Nashville, Tennessee. On the trip to Montgomery I thought about the possibility of continuing my musical career in Nashville. I liked Roy and all the people I had traveled with because they were just like folks back home, and I felt that I was part of a big family. However, it was obvious that the girl singers were being held back in their careers by men who would not let them get ahead. It was not hard to look around and see a lot of talented girls in Nashville who were not given the opportunity to advance according to their ability. I decided I would go to New York and continue my studies there.

I packed everything I owned into a trunk and boarded a train at Union Station in Montgomery headed for New York. I had been told by Elizabeth Lane from Montgomery about a respectable place for young girls to stay called the Rehearsal Club, so when I arrived in New York at Grand Central Station with my trunk I went to the brownstone building at 47 West 53rd Street. Its most famous prior resident was Carol Burnett. There was a housemother and an assistant housemother. They had Jamaican maids who did the housework. With your room came a continental breakfast and a full meal at suppertime. I ended up on the third floor sharing one bath with about fifteen girls. The room I shared with a girl from California was just large enough to hold two single beds and one dresser.

I liked the Rehearsal Club because of the requirement that all the girls who stayed there must be pursuing or studying for a career in the arts. There were two young girls from the Carolinas who were less than sixteen years of age who had been allowed to come to New York and study ballet by their parents. Some of the girls were Rockettes at Radio City Music Hall. Others were studying dance at the American School of Ballet or dramatics at the American Drama Institute. I took classes from Richard Edelman, who was an instructor in dramatic art at the Neighborhood Playhouse. I took diction lessons at the Betty Cashman Studio and voice lessons from Carlo Menotti. I had saved the money I made on the Roy Acuff tour, and my family footed the rest of my bill.

I had one friend already living in New York—Judy Justice, who had been a cheerleader with me at Sidney Lanier High School. A couple of months later Rachel decided to try her luck in the big city. Judy was modeling for an imported knitwear company and Rachel enrolled in the Collegiate Business Institute. Rachel, Judy and two other girls moved into a cold-water flat on the third floor of an apartment house. We met at lunch and went out at night together. We also found another Alabama friend, Leslie Blumberg, whose family owned the leading department store in Dothan, Alabama, near Elba. Leslie soon became our male escort for nights out in the city.

One night when Judy, Rachel and I were going to see a Broadway play we were rushing down Broadway to the theater

Two formal occasions:
"Being presented" by a proud
stepfather, Dr. Austin,
and being congratulated
by Mother after receiving
my first honorary doctorate.

when I looked ahead of me a few feet and saw Phil Everly with a girl at his side. Our eyes met but we passed without speaking. When we sat down in the theater the girls were saying how strange it is to pass someone you know in New York City, of all places. Then one of them happened to mention that it was September 25, Hank Williams Memorial Day, the day I had met Phil.

In between my classes I made all the auditions I could. I auditioned for the "Do-Re-Mi Show," and when they found out that I sang and played a guitar and wrote songs they allowed me to sing one of the songs that I had composed. I called Mother beforehand and she and her friends watched me in Montgomery. Many of them sent telegrams afterward. That was my first appearance on network television.

I sang on the Theodore Bikel Show as it was broadcast from the Village Gate. Theodore Bikel sang and emceed his own FM show and it was commonly known that he liked to give a new folksinger a break. A friend arranged for me to be on his show. The night I was to appear, the City of New York had become covered in snow and traffic was stalled. It was impossible for me to get transportation any closer than two or three blocks away from the place where I was supposed to perform. After tromping through the snow, I arrived at my destination only to find my feet were sopping wet and freezing cold from the slush I had waded through. I was afraid the dampness and wetness would give me a cold, so I removed my shoes, and when Theodore Bikel introduced me I walked on the stage barefoot. I didn't think that was out of key with my act since I was from a rural area in Alabama. I sang a folksong that I had written and Theodore Bikel interviewed me for a few minutes. Josh White, the noted black folksinger, was also on the show, with his daughter, who was making her debut as a singer.

After living in New York for several months, going to auditions and taking all those lessons, my money was running low so I took a job. The owner of Rachel's secretarial school got a job for me as a receptionist on the executive floor of Music Corporation of America. I didn't have enough money to buy her a gift, so I wrote a poem and sent it to her to express my gratitude. While working there I continued to make auditions and attend drama classes at night. I was told by the personnel director in the course of my preliminary interview that Mr. Jules Stein, board chairman of MCA, was a very conservative man with very conservative tastes. The women who worked for his organization were to wear clothes in keeping with the fashion he prescribed. The colors of dresses that were recommended for me to wear were gray, black, brown, beige—never anything in loud colors such as red. While I appreciated Mr. Stein's good taste, it didn't suit a girl with black hair and brown eyes. My wardrobe was filled with bright-colored clothes. As a matter of fact I could think of only two or three dresses I owned that would fit the required code of dress. I tried my best to dress in a conservative manner, but on occasions when my more subdued clothes were at the dry cleaner's I would occasionally have to slip into a colorful dress.

The only people who ever came on the executive floor of MCA besides the runners and two secretaries were Mr. Stein, Mr. Stein's brother-in-law the vice-president, and five executive vice-presidents who were also attorneys for the firm. It was on a day when I was forced, out of need, to wear a red dress to work that for the first time I came face to face with the owner of Music Corporation of America.

Mr. Stein stepped out of the elevator nattily dressed in a dark suit, and there I sat wearing a red dress. He had on a dark overcoat and was wearing gloves and a hat and carrying a cane. He took one disdainful look at me and marched over to the valuable oil painting that was hanging on the wall in the reception room. He straightened it and checked to see if it had been dusted. Then he marched back to his office. I have never since in all my life seen a man of his high station who was so particular down to the most minute detail of everything connected with him. When I learned that he had given up a brilliant career as an eye surgeon to enter the entertainment business, I realized that it was his surgical training that gave him a critical eye for detail in everything he did. It probably made him the tremendous success that he was.

One day while I was sitting at my tiny desk doing my work, word passed through the building that Charlton Heston was in the building. He came up to the executive floor and went into the conference lounge to sign some pictures. He called out and asked me if I could get some black ink for him to autograph the photographs. I told him I would try.

As soon as I hung up the phone I realized he had asked me to complete an impossible task. There is blue ink or blue-black ink, but rarely is black ink used by a secretary. Usually it is used only by a draftsman. I called around the building and found that what I suspected was true. When I told my dilemma to one of the men working for MCA someone went next door and tried to find some black ink at the drugstore. We were never able to come up with anything but the blue-black ink which I took to Mr. Heston. I told him I was sorry I could not find any black ink, and he said it really didn't matter, that he had already signed the photographs anyway.

Mr. Heston had caused quite a stir on some of the other floors by sitting down at one girl's typewriter and typing a message. I suspected that asking for the black ink and typing at the typewriter were probably just his gimmicks to make people talk about him after he left the building.

One day when I was at the drugstore lunch counter for a coffee break, I struck up a friendship with the soda jerk. He and I were talking and laughing and when I got up to pay my bill a young mustached man sitting next to me took my check and paid it. I didn't know him, but he told me his wife was from Tennessee and that his children were in private school in Tennessee.

The next day the soda jerk asked me if I knew the man who had paid for my Coke yesterday. He said it was Freddie Fields, Polly Bergen's agent husband, and that he was the tightest man in the whole Music Corporation of America. He said he had never seen him pay for even a cup of coffee for a friend. I surmised that my Southern accent must have made him feel at home.

Jerry Weintraub was one of the young agents working for MCA. Jerry was crazy about a country singer named Molly Bee who sang on the Tennessee Ernie Ford television show. Since his girl friend was seldom in New York, Jerry occasionally would ask me to go with him to check on some of the acts he booked for MCA.

206

One night I accompanied him to a Brooklyn theater where we paid a call on Bobby Darin. When we entered his dressing room backstage, Bobby, dressed in a blue jumpsuit with a holster on his hip and a pistol in his hand, was standing in front of a full-length mirror practicing quick draws. Jerry attempted to introduce me, but Bobby never took his eyes off his image in the mirror.

Jerry is married to Jaye P. Morgan and enjoys the reputation of being the top promoter in show business, working with such stars as Elvis Presley, Frank Sinatra and John Denver.

One night in April, 1960, when I was living in New York City, my mother and Charles called me from Montgomery and told me that my father had been taken to St. Margaret's Hospital in Montgomery with acute bronchitis. When we completed our conversation I called Daddy at the hospital. He said that he was feeling better, that the doctors had run a series of X rays and could find nothing wrong with him. The next morning they were going to take another X ray and would probably release him the next day. Three days later Mother called me back and said that my father had undergone surgery. They had found a spot and had removed a portion of his right lung. Mother said that I should come home immediately.

I didn't bother to pack any of my personal belongings but just grabbed a few things and caught the first plane back to Montgomery. When I arrived at St. Margaret's Hospital I walked into the room, and when I saw my father bandaged all around his chest and with a tube in his side, my knees turned to water and I almost fainted. The nurse who was in his room took me outside and brought some smelling salts to revive me. I was not mentally prepared to see him in this condition.

I waited for the two physicians who operated on him to make their rounds and I spoke to them in the hall outside Daddy's room. They told me that in the portion of his lung they had removed they had found the most highly malignant type of cancer known to man. The cancer cells were already in the rib bone they had removed to gain access to his lung. I knew of course that there was no cure for cancer and that if my father had a very highly malignant type there was no way he could survive this terrible disease. I asked the doctors how long they expected him to live. They told me—since there was no way to be sure—he could live six weeks or six months. I also asked them if they had told my daddy of the seriousness of his illness. They said they had not, and that in most cases people did not ask the direct question, "Do I have cancer?" They said if he did they would tell him the truth.

Daddy recovered from the surgery. The doctors said they would not allow him to suffer and that they would keep him sedated. We dismissed all the private duty nurses except the daytime shift. Daddy was very afraid since part of his lung had been removed that he would wake up in the night and not be able to get his breath. He asked me if I would stay in the room with him at night and call a nurse for him in case he needed some help.

For the entire duration of my father's hospitalization I slept on a folded cot in his room. In the morning I would get up, go home, bathe, put on a fresh dress and return to the hospital in the afternoon; then the daytime nurse would leave. Daddy did not really need round-the-clock nursing care, but it seemed to make him feel better having someone in the room with him. He never once mentioned the word cancer. Anytime his doctors would come in, he would say, "I hope you are not going to operate on me again." They would say they were not.

I never saw my daddy feeling any pain or discomfort. I never heard him complain. Gradually he was given a little morphine each day and he seemed to be satisfied and comfortable. He was able to get up out of his bed and get around. Perhaps because of the narcotic he was receiving, he never questioned the fact that he was not allowed to go home or be discharged from the hospital.

Daddy got thinner and thinner. One day the doctors told us they did not expect him to last through the night. His liver had become involved and early that morning he went into a coma. His brothers and sisters came to the hospital and sat with Charles and me all day. Late in the afternoon the nurse summoned all of us to come to my father's bedside. We crowded into his room and stood at the foot of his bed. He had not opened his eyes all that day. The nurse had told us that he was about to die. The nurse was checking his blood pressure and pulse. The end was near. Then right at the last minute he opened his eyes and looked down at the end of the bed at us and big tears filled his eyes. Then slowly they closed and he was dead.

My father's death was a terrible blow to me. As I watched his casket slowly lowered into the grave, the finality hit me like a bolt of lightning and reduced me to hysterical sobs. Being separated from my father when I was young was a traumatic experience but having him leave this world was sheer agony to endure.

I was twenty-one years old and I had now lost Granny, Uncle Carl, Uncle Ross and Daddy. Four people I loved deeply and who loved me in return. Now my father was gone and I felt tremendously lonely.

Chapter 16

AFTER MY FATHER'S DEATH, Dr. Austin, who was a member of the Kiwanis Club, asked me if I would go up to Camp Kiwanis, a new Girl Scout summer camp that the Montgomery Kiwanis Club sponsored on Lake Martin, and teach waterskiing. The camp was just opening for the first time. Dr. Austin, who had been Alabama Health Officer and past commander of the Alabama American Legion, was a great American and a patriot.

I accepted this job only with the stipulation that I would be able to commute to Montgomery and would not have to stay at night in the camp. It was a hangover from the old days when I went to camp after my Uncle Carl had died. I had become very homesick. They played taps, which reminded me of my uncle's funeral, and I cried myself to sleep every night. The counselors agreed to allow me to commute.

I taught 125 little girls who had never before water-skied. All the girls learned to ski except one who was too aggressive and kept pulling on the ropes and making herself fall.

At the end of the six weeks the camp held open house for the parents of the Girl Scouts and members of the Kiwanis Club. The girls and I were asked to put on a water show. With the two boats that we had, we did not have enough horsepower to pull up six girls, so we took up three on each boat, pulling six girls out behind. The girls passed the reviewing stands, waving and doing the skier's salute. The second time around three of them climbed and made a pyramid. For the closing act of the show I came around skiing backwards on one ski with my foot in the rope.

The feats we performed are astonishing only if you consider the fact that I had never before taught waterskiing. I had learned to instruct these girls from a comic book on waterskiing which I had gotten from the American Water Skiing Association. I did not have any trick skis but I had learned to ski backwards on two regular skis by sticking my head under the water and taking off underwater backwards.

In retrospect it is hard for me to see how I was able to accomplish so much with these children in such a short length of time, only having five or six of the girls for an hour every morning. None of the girls had more than fifteen minutes' ski time per day. If I had known the rewards and pleasures of teaching young children and the joy they experience the first time they learn any new skill, I am sure that I would have ended up in the teaching profession. Before then, being a performer, I never envisioned that I would find the satisfaction and pleasure in teaching I found that summer with those girls. I know they probably thought I had done a lot for them, but actually they had done much more for me by taking my mind off the sadness and loss of my father. It is one of the fondest memories of my life to think of the time with those young and fine girls at Camp Kiwanis.

In the fall when the camp closed I was living at home with mother and Dr. Austin. I took part in the Montgomery Little Theater productions of "A Streetcar Named Desire," "Lysistrata" and a Chinese production called "The Yellow Jacket." During the winter months, although I was active and busy, I lapsed into a period of despair and depression as a result of my father's death. I was not totally aware that I was experiencing such trauma except that, when I would eat, Mother would call my attention to the fact that I was staring into space.

In January, Mother agreed to be a volunteer worker for the local March of Dimes chapter. When the time came for her to make her Mothers' March, which was scheduled for seven one evening, several of her friends came by for an impromptu visit. Mother was not able to leave her guests to complete her charitable obligation. She came to me and said, "Cornelia, would you take the Mothers' March for me?"

"Yes, Mother, I would love to, but I am not a mother." Laughing, I took the collection bag from her hand and started my tour of the neighborhood houses. Our next-door neighbor on one side was Mrs. Anna D. Sawyer, who had come to Montgomery from Brewton, Alabama. Mrs. Sawyer was widowed and was rarely home, as she toured and traveled a great deal. I had never met her and could not remember ever seeing her at home. I decided to make her house the last house on the block, as I was certain she was not home anyhow. When I came to her house, I hesitated and then decided I would ring the doorbell. Much to my surprise Mrs. Sawyer came to the door. I solicited her for the March of Dimes drive and while we were talking she asked me if I liked to water-ski. I told her that I did and that I had taught waterskiing at Camp Kiwanis during the summer. She told me she was leaving the next day for Cypress Gardens, Florida, to visit her sister, Julie Pope, who was married to Dick Pope, the owner of Cypress Gardens. She asked me if I would like to water-ski for them. I told her I would like that very much. Not expecting to hear from Mrs. Sawyer, I told her good-bye and said I would see her when she returned to Montgomery.

Within three days I received a letter from Cypress Gardens asking for some photographs, with an enclosed application for employment at the Gardens. I filled out the application and sent the required photographs. I immediately received a reply from Cypress Gardens stating that I was accepted to water-ski, asking me when I could come and how long I thought I could stay. I sent a telegram saying that I could come immediately and could stay indefinitely. And that is exactly what I did.

I drove to Cypress Gardens and on the way down received the first and only speeding ticket in my life. It just so happened that my speedometer didn't work. Although I knew I was probably going over the speed limit, I thought I could dodge the ticket because my speedometer was broken. However, the highway patrolman who stopped me told me that was no excuse. I had to give him forty of the fifty dollars I had, right there on the road. I must admit it was quite a blow and I was too embarrassed and had too much pride to call my family and let them know I only had ten dollars to last me until my first paycheck, which was two weeks away.

I arrived at Cypress Gardens and took a room in the home

of a lady named Mrs. Laura Tucker. All the girls who skied at the Gardens were required to live in approved homes in town. Mrs. Tucker was a wonderful woman that I came to love and admire very much. There were six girls living in her home and we each paid her eight dollars per week for a place to sleep, but not for meals. Mrs. Tucker was so goodhearted that she invited us to eat supper with her anyhow. We in turn did chores for her around the house, such as cleaning and washing dishes, and also helped look after her fourteen-year-old daughter, Anna.

Simon Khoury was the director of the ski show. He was the taskmaster. He and I had a mutual admiration for each other mainly because we had one thing in common: We were both perfectionists. If Simon ever asked you why you made a mistake in the show and you offered him an explanation, he had one answer: "I accept no excuse." He ran a tight ship. I was eager to meet the strict standards he set.

I loved to water-ski and being at Cypress Gardens gave me a new outlook on life. It was like getting paid while you were on a summer vacation. I would probably have skied for nothing, I loved it so much. Cypress Gardens ran four shows a day, and in order to give all the skiers a chance to perform we were usually scheduled to ski in two or three shows a day. I would have loved to do four shows a day.

In between shows we sat in the Gardens in our antebellum gowns, waving to tourists and posing for photographs. I found this rather boring at first, but it soon became a source of much fun because we had many hours to let our imaginations run wild. We visited with many foreigners and tourists from every state in the Union. The antebellum costumes were allotted to the girls on a seniority basis, and since I was a new girl my costume was the least attractive of the lot. Wanting to look my best for the tourists, I decided I would make a costume to wear.

I bought some pink organdy material, and pink lace trim, and made a ruffled antebellum dress with matching gloves, a pocketbook, a broad-brimmed hat and a parasol. The photo department, which is one of the biggest departments at Cypress Gardens, was so impressed with the gown I had made that they asked if, rather than wear it, I would please present it to their department for photographs only. Before I terminated my employment with the Gardens I did present my gown to the photographic department.

The backward swan is the star act for a girl in the Cypress Gardens water-ski show. When a vacancy occurred I decided to try out for the position. Every morning I would arrive at the Gardens early for practice sessions and stay and practice after everyone had left. There were several girls competing, but when Simon finally called us to perform for him, I was the only one who had perfected the act.

I was allotted the coveted spot in the show. The backward swan is a balancing act that is done on one ski with a shoe mounted on a ball-bearing pivot that turns 180 degrees. You take off from the dock with your foot in the shoe in a standing position, then jump into the water. As the boat pulls you around you put your other foot in a toe-pull strap and you make the complete 180-degree turn skiing backward, being pulled by the other leg. You return to a front position and then, to complete the shore landing, you do a full swan, standing forward position, and land on the beach.

I had tried to reach stardom as a pianist, a country singer, a composer, and a summer-stock actress. Now I had finally reached stardom as a water-ballet queen—all because my mother had asked me to go on her round for the Mothers' March of Dimes. Many times I have been disappointed by not reaching my goals but just as often I have found success from opportunities I least expected.

My waterskiing career ended with a splash!

I skied six days a week for Cypress Gardens, the seventh day for myself if I had the opportunity. On one of my days off I was skiing with some friends when one of them suggested I try to ski barefooted. The American Water Ski Association had a very exclusive club for people who could ski on their bare feet for 100 yards. The membership roster listed less than ten girls. Two of those skied at the Gardens and were about my size. I wanted my name on that list and was confident that if they could ski barefooted, I could too.

My friends were amateurs and they gave me some inadequate instructions, forgetting the most important part of barefoot skiing, how to take the fall. I stepped off the freeboard and

I love the spray of the water and the wind in my hair.
This is how I won the Florida Sunshine Circuit.

hit the water going about fifty miles an hour. It felt like I had hit a brick wall. I was dazed but the breath was not knocked out of me. When my friends suggested I try again, I thought they must be crazy but resolved the next time I would make it. The second spill was just as bad as the first. The force of the water popped my neck backward. I didn't go for the third try because I knew I might never live to talk about it.

At the time I didn't know I had sustained any injury, but gradually my neck became so stiff I wasn't able to lift my arms over my head to put on a dress. A doctor diagnosed my condition as costochondritis, a temporary arthritis, and advised that I no longer ski professionally.

While I was skiing at Cypress Gardens I met and married John Snively III. John was a third-generation Floridian and a member of a citrus-growing family. His grandfather, John Snively, Sr., had come to Winter Haven in the early days and had pioneered the citrus industry, establishing many of the cooperatives that were formed in the surrounding area. Tom and Pete, two of his brothers, followed him to Florida. The efforts of the three Snively brothers at one time produced one tenth of the world's supply of citrus. I had two sons, Jim and Josh Snively, before my marriage ended tragically in divorce seven years later, in 1969.

In the spring of 1962 I had come back home to Montgomery to prepare for my wedding to John Snively. Uncle Jimmy was in the midst of his third campaign for governor. His chief opponents were George Wallace, who was making his second bid, and a very attractive dark-horse candidate, Ryan DeGraffenreid. One day I went down to the local Folsom headquarters to work and was told there was nothing to do. Another time I went to pick up some literature and was told the pamphlets were locked up and the man who had the key wasn't around. I had an uneasy feeling that something was amiss in the Folsom camp. I attended several rallies but the old punch in Uncle Jimmy's speeches was gone and the organization was loose. However, the *National Observer* had picked Uncle Jimmy to win and we felt confident he would be elected in spite of his slipshod organization.

A few days before the election I heard that the odds in

Uncle Jimmy stumping
the state in 1962.

A typical flyer for
a Folsom campaign.

Las Vegas were heavily in favor of George Wallace. That was the first time I had ever heard of wholesale gambling over a governor's race. I refused to believe that the odds were an accurate projection of the voters' preference in Alabama.

On the eve of the election Dr. Austin, Mother and I stayed home to watch Uncle Jimmy make his last pitch on television. Thirty minutes before the broadcast there was a loud, frantic pounding at our front door. When we opened the door, there to our surprise was Melissa, trembling and crying. In between hysterical sobs she said over and over, "They've done something to my daddy."

After she quieted down she related the series of events that had unnerved her. Some weeks before Uncle Jimmy had made a television tape to be aired from Birmingham the night before the election. Early in the afternoon someone discovered the film had gotten wet. No one offered any acceptable explanation but nevertheless the film was ruined. It was too late to make another tape. Uncle Jimmy would have to go on live. Uncle Jimmy wanted to televise from Birmingham, but for some reason he was told he would have to go to a television station in Montgomery. His wife and children were to be seated with him during the telecast. By midafternoon the entourage had arrived at the Holiday Inn West in Montgomery. About an hour before time to depart for the television studio, Melissa went to her father's room only to be denied admission by a man standing outside his door. Melissa, who was twenty years old at the time and the oldest child at home now that Rachel was married and living in New Jersey, demanded to see her father. When her demands were refused, she suspected something was wrong and tried to bolt past the guard at the door, whereupon she was bodily restrained. This confirmed her suspicions and out of desperation she had fled to us. Melissa's emotional state was such that we were distracted from making any sense out of the story.

By the time Melissa had calmed down enough to tell us what had happened, it was time for Uncle Jimmy's telecast. The announcer introduced Uncle Jimmy and the camera showed Uncle Jimmy and Jamelle and their children, except for Melissa and Rachel. When Uncle Jimmy tried to call each child by name he fumbled and failed, obviously confused. He groped and searched for words that would not form on his lips. The picture on our television set turned completely upside down three separate times, a mechanical feat that can only be achieved by the cameraman flipping the lens on the camera back and forth (certainly no accident). This visual effect plus Uncle Jimmy's inability to name his own children equaled total confusion. He finally rambled off some nonspecific monologue, and when he finished there was no doubt he was finished politically.

We sat staring at the television set with blank expressions on our faces. Stunned and dismayed, we said nothing, for we all knew the inevitable. There was no way to erase that picture from the minds of the voters.

The next day Mother, Dr. Austin and I went to the polls wishing for the world we could go unnoticed lest someone ask us to explain the television catastrophe. I tried to conjure up a fantasy. Two flickered in my mind. "Everybody in Alabama went to the movies last night" or "Every television set in the state went on the blink."

Several loyal friends approached us as we left the polls. "What on earth happened to Big Jim?" they asked with grave concern. As it turned out, those people who didn't see the ill-fated television show heard about it. Before the polls closed on Election Day the talk had spread over the state and Uncle Jimmy ran third, DeGraffenreid second, and George Wallace first. DeGraffenreid was defeated in the runoff and George Wallace was elected to his first term as Governor of Alabama.

We believe that Uncle Jimmy was drugged that night, that the pretaped film was sabotaged, that the television cameraman was paid to turn the picture upside down and that it was an inside job! The drug given was so powerful Uncle Jimmy's blood pressure shot up and a blood vessel ballooned in his brain, causing him to pass out on the steps of the television station as he was leaving the studio. Some time later he passed out again from the same enlarged blood vessel. This time he stopped breathing and Melissa gave him mouth-to-mouth resuscitation until he was rushed to the hospital. The aneurism was discovered and surgically corrected, leaving Uncle Jimmy partially blind in one

219

eye. His physicians said that whatever caused his blood pressure to skyrocket would have undoubtedly killed him if he had been a normal-sized man.

The man who barred Melissa's entrance to her father's room was appointed to a judgeship and the cameraman was appointed to a state board, although neither one had previously been employed by the state of Alabama or held public office.

My wedding went on as planned but Uncle Jimmy was unable to attend. Rachel and Melissa and Bama were in the wedding, and Jamelle came with some of the other children.

Chapter 17

AFTER MY DIVORCE I decided to live in Montgomery since all of my relatives live in Alabama and I felt a tremendous need for the security and comfort of being close to my family.

Back in Montgomery it was politics as usual in the capital city. My sons, Jim and Josh, were five and six years old and had not been exposed to the atmosphere of Southern politics in which I grew up. I wanted them to appreciate their political heritage, so at the first opportunity I took them to an old-fashioned political rally. George Wallace was the main speaker and he had brought along his youngest daughter, Lee. As I watched little Lee sitting so poised on the platform, I thought how lonely she must have become since her mother had died. My heart went out to her and in a gesture of compassion I took Jim and Josh over to speak to her.

It was just a fleeting moment in a crowd of people but Lee must have sensed the warm feeling I had for her. Her need for a mother was evidently greater than anyone had realized because after the rally she told her daddy that she wanted him to marry "that lady with the black hair and the two little boys." My courtship with George might have started at that point only Lee forgot my name and George couldn't figure out which lady she was talking about.

Some time later my brother, Charles, was in Montgomery spending the weekend with me. He had come up from Elba to participate in a National Guard drill. I had started to cook supper for Charles when he told me he planned to eat with George Wallace. He had been invited to the Wallace home by one of his Guard buddies, Jim Parsons, who was married to George's oldest daughter, Bobbie Jo.

"Can't you get me an invitation?" I asked.

"I don't think it would be proper for me to ask," Charles said.

"Here I am single and George Wallace is widowed and you won't even help me get a date. You didn't even get me a date when we were in high school," I prodded.

"You never seemed to have any trouble getting dates without my help," Charles reminded me.

"No thanks to you," I said.

Charles refused to be chided into playing the role of Cupid, so I stayed home and Charles went to eat at the Wallaces'.

Montgomery is very much like an overgrown small town. There are very few unattached men in the city who happen to be near my age. Most of the men fall into "two" unacceptable categories: "too" young or "too" married. I was psychologically blind to George Wallace because he had been married ever since I had known him. I had never thought of him as anything but a political candidate and a long-time friend of the family. Now that he was virtually the most eligible man in town, I began to think of him in a different way.

George and I had many friends in common, all of whom were not as reluctant as my brother to try their hand at matchmaking. Ruth and Will Waller made the first overture to match George and me. The Wallers invited me to dinner and extended an invitation to George and another single man. The other gentleman showed up but George shied off when he realized what Ruth had in mind.

My next-door neighbors, Sue and Tom Johnson, were successful in getting George and me together for dinner the first time. However, George spent the entire evening wooing potential votes from a handful of nonsupporters. Undoubtedly he was more interested in political pursuits than romantic pursuits.

Charles finally came back for another Guard drill weekend. This time I insisted he invite Bobbie Jo and Jim to eat with us. Someone suggested (probably me) that we ask George to join

A wish come true: flying the F-4 jet fighter.

us. Bobbie Jo made the call and George accepted. His motive for coming was not altogether apolitical. George had just defeated my Uncle Jimmy in the first primary of the 1970 governor's race. Uncle Jimmy entered every governor's race after 1962, although he had little chance of winning. He just loved the action. George trailed Albert Brewer, who was finishing the term of George's wife, the late Governor Lurleen Wallace. George needed all the help he could get to beat Brewer in the upcoming runoff. George wanted a public endorsement from Jim Folsom, and he asked me to speak to my uncle in his behalf.

George began calling me to talk politics. He never got the endorsement he was seeking from my uncle but he never stopped calling. I didn't think George was seriously interested in me but needless to say I was flattered by his attention.

Our political conversations became more and more personal. We talked for long periods of time about everything under the sun. Mostly George talked about his deceased wife and I talked about my ex-husband. The conversations became somewhat like therapy sessions for both of us. We talked of marriage. When we finally talked about marrying each other George would say, "You don't want to marry me, someday I'll be in a wheelchair. . . ." And I always answered, "That wouldn't bother me because I'm looking for a man who can't get away."

When I realized I had fallen in love with George I tried to analyze why I was so attracted to him. His attitudes and physical features were very much like those of my father, his sense of humor was similar to that of my Uncle Ross and his ambitions and political drive equaled that of my Uncle Jimmy. In essence he was every man I had ever loved all in one.

By the same token George felt comfortable with me. He had watched me grow up and he knew everything about me and my family. Through me he was able to identify with his earliest days in politics. He found a security in knowing me well, since he hesitated to trust the motives of people he had become acquainted with since he had become governor.

Finally, George invited me to have Sunday dinner with him and his children. Lee was there, and after I left she took her daddy aside and exclaimed, "Daddy, that's her! That's the lady with the two boys, the one I want you to marry."

224

Naturally, George was concerned about how the public would react to his remarriage, since his wife had been governor and so revered by the people of Alabama. I was more concerned with our children's happiness and whether or not the marriage would be acceptable to them.

With our children's blessings George and I were married on January 4, 1971. Dr. Robert Strong performed the quiet religious ceremony at the Trinity Presbyterian Church in Montgomery. Only members of our family were present. George and I were still enjoying the blissful ecstasy of an extended honeymoon when he embarked on the whirlwind presidential campaign of 1972. I was a bride of only one year and four months when my husband was suddenly gunned down in Laurel, Maryland, on May 15, 1972.

Chapter 18

GEORGE SPENT the rest of the summer of 1972 at the Spain Rehabilitation Center in Birmingham. Jim and Josh had already gone to Florida to spend the summer with their father. Lee was staying with Bobbie Jo in Birmingham. George, Jr., was either at our beach house or at the Mansion in Montgomery. Peggy Sue continued to keep her vigil with me at the hospital.

Dr. George A. Hallenbeck, who was chief of general surgery at the University of Alabama and who had performed the gall-bladder surgery on President Johnson, opened and drained the abscess that was discovered in Miami. George was extremely concerned over having to submit to additional surgery. Dr. Hallenbeck tried to quiet his fears by repeating an anecdote from President Johnson. He said that before he operated on President Johnson, the President had told him, "It would not help the reputation of a physician to have a dead president on his hands." George was amused but nevertheless reluctant to undergo another operation.

Several days after the wounds from the new surgery began to close George was introduced to a new physical therapy program. It was along the same lines as the program that he had had in Maryland but more extensive. The goal of rehabilitation medicine is to make the paraplegic totally independent. George learned more complicated routines such as transferring from his wheelchair, taking charge of his morning bath habits, learning to dress himself, and putting on his braces alone. His

226

physical therapy program was broadened from parallel bars to weight lifting, overhead pulls and balancing exercise. He was introduced to occupational therapy and placed in a standing box for an hour each day. My comment on that phase of the program was, "I didn't know anyone offered job training for governors." The golden rule was for George to push his wheelchair unassisted. George learned everything except how to drive a car, which was probably a blessing since he never was a very good driver anyhow and he had hardly driven at all since his first term as governor in 1963.

The rehab people expected George to throw himself into the new routine as if he were in training for a boxing match; so did I. We were sorely disappointed. He went through the motions of the exercises but never with any real enthusiasm. The additional surgery hindered his progress before he got started. The four walls of the hospital room seemed to close in on him and he lost interest in everything. Realizing that he was becoming more and more depressed, I again approached Dr. Traugh about the possibility of staying in the hospital, all to no avail. The goal of the program is to make the patient totally independent, an impossible task if a family member is constantly doing the things for a patient he should be doing himself.

Dr. Traugh was not being unreasonable; it just happened to be standard procedure for the rehabilitation center to strictly regulate visiting hours. The patients spent four hours a day in therapy sessions and family members tended to interfere with this schedule, as well as tiring the patients when they needed to be resting. Being too emotionally involved and not objective, families sometimes viewed the program as cruel and frequently objected to the treatment of their loved ones. Families tend to overprotect the spinal-cord-injured person and hinder his progress in the program. Separation of family and patient is supposed to motivate the patient to complete the therapy program so he can return to his home.

Although I was sympathetic with the established rules I was too worried about George to be concerned with the theories of rehabilitation medicine.

My own reserves were running low and I knew if George

sank into a deep depression I would not have the strength to pull him out of it. I felt a sense of desperation. By virtue of the fact that George was governor of the state he was also chairman of the Board of Trustees of the University of Alabama. Finally I went over Dr. Traugh's head and took my problem to the head of the University Hospital, Dr. Richardson Hill. I told him I was so concerned over George's mental attitude that I felt if they could not make arrangements for me to stay in my husband's room I would have to remove George from the hospital. Dr. Hill was equally concerned over George's mental state. The next day a sofa was placed in George's room and I slept there every night for the remainder of his hospitalization.

I have no way of knowing how much it helped George, but it helped me tremendously to be near him. I stayed out of the room in the mornings and busied myself with chores while he was in therapy. In the afternoons and evenings, I stayed in his room and only assisted when he would have called a nurse anyhow.

Within a few weeks Dr. Hallenbeck discovered yet another abscess. Once again the physical therapy routine was interrupted and he was taken to the University Hospital, where the second abscess was opened and drained. Given a few days to recover he was then back into his regular exercise program.

George didn't set any records but Dr. Traugh felt he had accomplished his rehabilitation program better than many twenty-year-old patients, especially considering the setbacks he experienced from the two abscess operations. Certainly what we both learned about the spinal-cord-injured patient was invaluable.

By the end of August all the children were back home and getting ready to start school. A few days before George was to be released from the Spain Rehabilitation Center I went home to Montgomery. It has been a custom with me to do something special with my children the night before school starts. Jim, Josh and Lee decided that they wanted to go roller-skating. I did not feel up to the loud music and noisy crowds of the skating rink so I tried to beg off, preferring to stay home and play a quiet game of tennis with some friends. The children insisted and not wanting to disappoint them I consented. I loved and enjoyed skating with them anyhow. I decided perhaps it would do me more good than the quiet evening I had planned.

Never satisfied with the ordinary way of doing things I decided to transfer the backward-swan skiing trick to roller-skating. I ended up with a broken leg. The children were very upset and felt guilty because they had insisted that I go roller-skating. When we arrived back at the Mansion we learned that someone had fired a gun over the back fence of the grounds and directly across the tennis court at almost the exact time I had broken my leg at the skating rink. I doubt that I would have been struck by the bullet but, given the nervous state I was in, the shock, I believe, would have caused me to have a heart attack. When George arrived home the next day from the Spain Rehabilitation Center I greeted him at the Mansion door on crutches.

The transition from hospital to home required George to make one adjustment he was not ready to accept—giving up his nurses. He had had the very best nurses since May, and by August he had become overly dependent on the figure in the white uniform. A nurse present in the room seemed to give him a sense of security. George's doctors felt that private-duty nurses were not in the best interests of his complete rehabilitation and advised that his home life should be as normal as possible in every way. They recommended that George terminate all nursing care upon his discharge from the hospital.

George declared he would rather stay in the hospital than go home without a nurse. Wanting him home so badly, I made a private pact with him, promising a nurse would be on duty when he arrived at the Mansion. Then I went about the business of devising a plan that would obey the doctor's orders as well as satisfy my husband's psychological needs. As soon as George settled into the bed at the Mansion he asked to see the living proof of my pledge. I told him that a nurse was in the next room waiting, elaborating that she was very nervous because this was the first time she had ever nursed a governor. I cautioned him to be considerate because she was young and inexperienced. Then I went into a prolonged detailed description of her physical attributes, telling him that she was blond, blue-eyed and just under five feet tall.

"Dispense with the rigamarole and let's see her," he challenged, doubting I could produce a nurse if I were a genie from a magic lamp.

I stepped to the door and in a very professional voice called, "The Governor would like to see you now."

In she walked, wearing her white nurse's uniform and cap, white stockings and shoes. George believed the scheme halfway across the room; then he reached for his glasses and recognized his daughter Peggy Sue. He gave us all a look of "I've been had" and laughed. Peggy Sue admirably nursed her father for several days, bringing his medications and taking his temperature. He agreed with me that she was the prettiest nurse he had the whole time he was sick.

Many of the people who worked on the staff at the Mansion were seeing George at close range for the first time. The last time they had seen him leave the Mansion he was a vibrant man on his way to a rally at a Maryland shopping center. They tried to meet him with a cheery greeting, but it was obvious that they were fighting to keep the Governor from seeing the sadness they felt over the tragedy that had befallen him.

Edward Maxwell, one of our black inmates, was not able to keep the tears from streaming down his face. Eyes glistening with tears, he shook his head, bowed it, turned and walked away to grieve in privacy. Edward had begun taking a personal interest in the Governor before he was injured. George had a habit of letting his food get cold while he read the paper, so Edward made a point of encouraging him to eat his meals while they were hot. We decided to let Edward take over the Governor's personal care. This proved to be a boon for us. Edward learned all the Governor's therapy program. He learned about the medication, braces and exercises and was instrumental in regulating his morning routine after he returned to the Mansion.

Adjusting our home life around a paraplegic was not easy. The temptation was great for all of us to do things for him rather than allow him to do things for himself. If he wanted something we fetched it. If he needed something we got it. Everyone was at his beck and call. We were destroying the man. Rehabilitation had taught me that George must be independent, and yet we all loved him so much and wanted so to help him recover that we were doing everything for him. We thought we were helping him when in fact we were only holding back his recovery. I knew that feeling helpless also made George feel worthless. I knew if he was going to have his self-esteem restored he needed to be as independent as possible.

I finally took a good look at the situation that was going on in the Mansion and decided to take measures to force George to be more independent. I spoke to the Mansion staff and the Governor's security people, asking them to try and restrain themselves from assisting him in any way unless it was absolutely necessary. The first and most important thing was to allow him to push his wheelchair. Since I seemed to be the only one who would say no to a governor, I accompanied George to work every day to make sure no one pushed his wheelchair.

The real villain was self-pity and George was drowning in it. George wanted sympathy and pity. Neither had been prescribed by his physicians and certainly would not be beneficial to his long-range recovery. When George lapsed into moods of feeling sorry for himself, I would simply tell him that it was hard for me to feel sorry for him. He had a college education, a law degree, he had been governor of the state twice, he still had a job, he had run for president, and he presently had the support and love of millions of people all over the country. There was no way, I told him, that I could feel sorry for a man who was so successful in life.

Eventually I ran out of reason and logic. My witty words waned and my collection of clever comedies collapsed. I was spent! I couldn't think of one cheerful thing to say.

Then one day when George was feeling particularly bad, some lines from an old hymn came to me from out of the blue. I slapped George on the back, threw back my head and sang in my loudest voice:

> "Cheer up my brother;
> Walk in the sunshine;
> We'll understand it all by and by."

I hadn't heard that song in years. I didn't even know the name of the hymn and I couldn't remember any of the other words to the song. God sent me that phrase just when I needed it most, and it carried a message that George needed to hear. I guess I sang it a hundred times after that.

Another problem to deal with was self-image. Being crippled made George feel stripped of his masculinity. For the first time since we had been married he started calling me "Mama," and I was still a bride of less than two years. I knew it was not in keeping with the character of the man I had married. It took me a while to realize George was rejecting his role of husband for that of an infant. He expected me to play mother and pamper him. If I had entered this game with him I could have made him dependent on me for life. He would have become emotionally crippled as well as physically crippled. In my eyes George was no different from what he was before he was shot. Some days I even forgot he couldn't get up out of the bed and walk! He was still the George Wallace I loved, married and desired and I refused to change my role as his wife.

At one point George became so lax in his routine that he was almost immobile, refusing to get up in the morning and staying away from the office. Dr. Hamilton H. Hutchinson, George's personal physician and devoted friend, had taken over George's case using the Veterans Administration nurses and technicians. With Dr. Hutchinson's approval, the Veterans Administration Hospital sent two of its finest rehabilitation nurses to Montgomery to work with George for a couple of weeks, one from Chicago and one from New York. It developed into a comical scene. Every morning they would come into our room and bodily drag George from the bed, put him in his wheelchair and start him into his program. After a morning of therapy and lunch they would plan his afternoons.

The following was a typical scene:

One of the nurses asked, "What would you like to do today, Governor?"

George replied, "Nothing."

The nurse insisted, "Oh, yes, you must do something."

"No," he said, "I don't want to do anything," and he hung his head, moaned and groaned with the pain in his side.

The other nurse joined in. "You can't just sit here and moan and groan all afternoon."

He looked straight at the woman, his eyes bright with fire, and through his clenched teeth he said, "Yes, I can. I am going to sit here and moan and groan."

The sergeants, as George affectionately called them, paid

232

Me and my friend Martha Mitchell.

"Cheer up my brother . . ."

no mind to what he said. They pushed George out of the house and took him downtown and the three of us sat in the barbershop while he got a haircut he did not need.

One day George looked at the two women and said, "As the Governor of this state, I'm commander in chief of the whole Alabama National Guard and I used to order around nineteen thousand men; now I can't even tell two sergeants what to do." The idea of their program was to motivate George and keep him active. It really didn't matter what he did as long as we kept him in motion.

The pain turned out to be the biggest problem of all, mainly because it was never-ending. For a while George became psychologically dependent on the pain injections, but when it became obvious he was asking for the shots too often, sterile water was substituted for the medicine and he never noticed the difference. Actually, he was trying to avoid facing the paralysis, which he was not yet able to accept. The injections were soon stopped altogether. We consulted with physicians all over the country trying to find some way to alleviate pain that was almost disabling. Dr. Hutchinson helped in every way he could, spending many hours of his family time in encouraging visits with George. He assisted us in our search for some relief for the pain. Under medical supervision George was given spinal injections of Xylocaine, with only temporary results. Then he tried an external electronic stimulator designed to block the pain impulses before they reached the brain. For a while this seemed to give George some relief, but unfortunately it did not last long. If he had taken any type of narcotic for very long the effectiveness of the medicine would eventually wear off and would no longer help. I rejected that solution to the pain problem as emphatically as did George's physicians.

We finally decided that we had nothing to lose by trying acupuncture. The medical doctors were skeptical, but they agreed to go along with us.

Although the acupuncture treatments were not beneficial to George, I do believe they are helpful to some people, particularly those suffering from arthritis and bursitis. The University of Alabama Hospital has since initiated a research program, and of the patients receiving acupuncture 60 percent report positive results.

234

George never asked for and never received any psychiatric treatment. None was recommended. However, since I found myself dealing with a problem about which I had no previous knowledge or experience, I consulted my cousin, Dr. James Folsom, Veterans Administration Psychiatrist in Rehabilitation, and Dr. Patrick Linton, head of psychiatry at the University of Alabama. They advised me on various problems associated with paraplegia. Many things I learned by reading and from experimentation.

I learned I had contributed in my own way to George's pain problem. Every time he grunted, I put my arms around him and kissed him, thinking I was giving him some comfort. I should have remembered my psychology course better than that. I had enforced his problem by rewarding him for his pain. I was advised to turn a deaf ear or leave the room whenever he began to complain.

Like most people I have a lot of empathy and I could not turn a deaf ear to my loved one's suffering, real or imagined. I had no choice but to leave the room. When I did, George would only go downstairs and seek out Mrs. Cain or Joanne to find sympathy. I asked Mrs. Cain and Joanne not to indulge him and they obliged. However, I knew it would be impossible for me to keep George from getting sympathy because he was too exposed to the public and there was plenty of sympathy out there whenever he asked for it. I never doubted that George had real pain. I only suspected he was using it rather than coping with it. When I was in the room with him he would complain. As soon as I walked out he would watch television, relaxed and comfortable. This is not to say that George did not have real pain. Anyone who has spinal-cord injury or any other type of back injury experiences some pain for the rest of their lives. There's only one way and that is to tolerate the pain and live with it. I tried my best to correct the mistake that I had made, although I am not sure I was ever completely successful.

The children noticed the change in George and it was hard for them to accept: a once-vital man, head of the family, now a complaining, moaning parent. The public never saw this side of George and I suppose that is why the family was his chosen audience. It seemed that when he was around anyone he loved, he could let down his guard.

Our mealtimes became most unpleasant. We were used to a man who came bouncing in from the office with a cheerful greeting and an affectionate hug for each of us. As head of the family he had always led our prayer and initiated the conversations at the dinner table. He would call for his mail and scan several newspapers before rushing back to work. Now we had before us a silent figure, holding his sides, head bowed, not out of respect for the Lord but from pain. Sometimes he wasn't even aware that we had said the blessing. He had little appetite, and if he ate at all, he picked at the food on his plate. This created a strain in the kitchen—the cook thinking he didn't like the food and changing the menus constantly, but failing each time to tempt his palate. For a while he existed on a diet of raw oysters.

The children were perplexed by George's behavior. They were too young to understand any psychological terminology I might offer for the change in his disposition. Rather than explain or make excuses, I decided to include them in trying to bring George out of himself.

The children were great through it all, going to any length to try to make the situation better. We would make up games to try to stimulate George's interest in family and food. They solved the mealtime problem in their own inventive way. One night at supper after we had said the blessing, the children all sat silently with their heads bowed, holding their sides. No one moved or said a word until George raised his head and started laughing. The children had mirrored their father's behavior. This method proved to be more beneficial than words ever could have in giving him an insight into how his problem was affecting us. George began to be more considerate of his family, and if he didn't feel well enough to sit up and participate at mealtime he stayed away from the table so that he wouldn't ruin the fellowship for the rest of us. Nothing changed overnight but slowly, as George improved, everything got better.

There was one particular incident that was evidence to me that George had forgotten his own personal miseries and had renewed his interest in the world around him. We were attending a banquet where George was the scheduled main speaker. The after-dinner entertainment was to be performed by the reigning Miss Alabama. Before an audience of three hundred and a bright-eyed, grinning Governor she demonstrated the talent that had won her the coveted title—an exotic hula dance in a native grass skirt. At the conclusion of her dance she placed a lei around George's neck and kissed him. At that moment if anyone had mentioned the word pain he would have said, "Window?"

When George stood up to make his talk he began his remarks by saying, "Honey, if you had done that dance for me while I was sick I would have gotten out of the hospital two months earlier." If I had known during all those long months I spent sitting in hospitals that a three-minute dance could produce an instant cure for my ailing husband I would have fetched the fair lass and beat the Congo drums while she gyrated her hips. The most remarkable thing about the whole incident was that Miss Alabama was a dedicated Christian who had overcome the crippling effects of polio.

After that I knew George was a well man. I continued to give him all the love and emotional security he needed at home but I no longer felt it was necessary for me to follow one step behind his wheelchair every time he made a personal appearance.

George's real salvation was his work. He made his personal appearances and went to his office regularly. When the Legislature came back into session they assembled in joint session for an address by the Governor. We had carefully chosen this time for George to make his debut in the standing box. When George, unaided, dramatically pulled himself to a full standing position there wasn't a dry eye in the house. His speech was applauded and cheered, but the real applause was for the man who through his own determination and faith in God, the love of his family and friends, the help of a lot of good doctors and the prayers of many people had made a miraculous comeback.

The road to recovery is not smooth. It is like a jagged line on a stock-market report. There are ups and downs until eventually when enough time has passed a full recovery is made. Time is a great healer of all wounds, physical and psychological, but until a certain amount of time passes no healing takes place. George's complete recovery took two years. It was not easy for anyone, least of all him. He was the one who had paid the highest price. He was the one who ultimately had to travel the long road to recovery.

I believe that what happened to George was part of God's plan in his life. There were many people who hated George Wallace before he was shot. There are many people who still do not agree with him politically, but the barriers of hatred were broken that day in Laurel, Maryland. Today for the first time in his national political career people who before had turned a deaf ear to the voice of George Wallace listen to what the man has to say. They may not agree but they are no longer deaf to his voice. I don't know if George will ever walk again. If he does it will be a miracle. I believe one thing: If George is ever the recipient of God's complete healing power, it will only be when God alone can claim the glory. If he never walks again he may serve God better by continuing to be an inspiration to millions of handicapped people—and to those of us who are able-bodied but are not measuring up to the tasks God has assigned us. George has shown us all by his example that with determination and faith in God we can mount any summit.

I had only been married to George one year and four months when he was shot down in Laurel, Maryland. I am sure that if I had known before I married him that I would have to experience the tragedy and sadness I have been through I would have turned and run the other way. But God had already shaped and molded my life. He had prepared me by allowing me to experience enough sadness, sorrow and heartbreak when I was young to be able to meet the hour that lay ahead. He gave me the strength to overcome the early setbacks in my life, and those victories gave me the confidence and courage to face this last tragedy when it came.

George and I both dedicated our lives to Christ long ago. We know that God has the power to change the course of our lives and take us in the direction that he wants us to go. We may end up in the White House in Washington or we may find ourselves living in a log cabin in Elba. We've placed our lives in higher hands and where we go from here is up to him.

In every bad thing that happens to us there is some good. The most precious time for me was one day when George poured out his heart to me. He told me how very much he

Driving the pace car at Talladega Speedway in 1973.

George and me—spanning twenty-eight years of
Alabama history and six inaugurations—in 1975.

loved me and that he couldn't have made it without me. He told me how much he appreciated all I had done for him.

For the first time he said to me what every wife wants to hear her husband say. I was the happiest and most satisfied I had ever been. I felt a deep and total contentment that only comes with the security of true love.

As a result of the terrible ordeal we had lived through, George had a new appreciation of life and a greater awareness of people and their needs.

The tragedy affected each of us in a different way. I've always called politics the "king of sports." I was born in it, I lived in it all my life and I've loved every minute of it. Now I find I've lost my enthusiasm for the campaign.